Through theatre and art, Good Chance creates new kinds of communities, empowering artists from across the world and connecting people, stories and cultures.

Founded by British playwrights Joe Murphy and Joe Robertson, Good Chance established its first temporary theatre of hope, an 11m geodesic dome, in the heart of the refugee and migrant camp in Calais in September 2015, promoting freedom of expression, creativity and dignity for everyone. It has since travelled to London's Southbank for a nine-day festival led by refugees in July 2016, and opened its doors to refugees, artists and local Parisians in the French capital for eight weeks in spring 2017, in collaboration with Collectif MU and Théâtre de la Ville, and for ten weeks in spring 2018 in collaboration with humanitarian NGO Emmaüs Solidarité. At the invitation of the Mayor of Paris, the Good Chance dome will return to the French capital in summer and autumn 2018. Alongside the dome theatres, the company creates groundbreaking productions and works with a collective of artists from across the world through the Good Chance Ensemble, most recently supporting the creation of the album *Sounds of Refuge* by John Falsetto and Mohamed Sarrar, recorded at Abbey Road Studios.

Good Chance is an Associate Company of the Young Vic Theatre and recipient of the Evening Standard Editor's Award (2016), an Empty Space Peter Brook Award (2017) and the Genesis Award (2018).

'I really thank the people who organise this great theatre. And we will know many things by it. For example, show different cultures, different people with different mind and language as well. So it doesn't matter how you look like, just be the best version of yourself.

Just come to the theatre. Even you will get knowledge from it.

Follow your ideas. Don't follow the other people ideas. Your mind is the best mind. And don't care what they're saying. Once again, thanks for the people who organised – God bless you.'

Alsadig from Sudan, fifteen years old,
a regular visitor to Good Chance Calais

'The refugee who sits alone, he does not just need food, or some materials, he needs also hope. Good Chance Theatre gives hope. You need to feel you are not alone, you need to feel someone sits beside you, he cares about you.'

Tarek, from Syria,
a regular visitor to Good Chance Paris

'A varied programme of music, drama, poetry, movement and debate, for and by the inhabitants of the camp, occupies the Good Chance theatre six days a week. All by itself it proclaims that life without culture is nothing but biology in survival mode. That was the lesson we brought home.'

Sir Tom Stoppard, *Sunday Times*

Good Chance Supporters

For their support of *The Jungle* we would like to thank:

All the team at the Young Vic and National Theatre, the KT Wong Foundation, Karen Bastick-Styles and the students and staff at Greenside School and The Elliot Foundation, Giulio Piscitelli, Jeffrey Culpepper and Susan Witherow, Refugees at Home, and all the individuals who participated in the development of the production; Raphael Acloque, Majid Adin, Jude Akuwudike, Albaraa Alhalabieh, Girum Bekele, Jack Bradley, Rob Callender, Ben Cooper, Nicole Charles, Mike Cunningham, Andy De La Tour, Sharief Dorani, Jack Ellis, Amir El-Masry, Yolli Fuller, Annie Gavrilescu, Sue Gladys Harvey, Michael Gould, Baraa Halabieh, Richard Hansell, Faisal Harbi, Ben Harrison, Paul Hilton, Tarek Iskander, Ansu Kabia, David Lan, Amra Mallassi, Adam Mohammedean Khamees, Hamed Moradi, Charles Mnene, Conor Neaves, Anthony Newton, Con O'Neill, Francesca Reidy, Sophie Stanton, Jane Suffling, Alex Sutton, Bernie Whittle and everyone at the National Theatre New Work Department.

For their time, wisdom and support since we first built our theatre in Calais in 2015 we would like to thank:

Louise Bernard, Joey Borgogna, Tiphaine Bouniol, Inda Bunyan, Stuart Burns, Cyril Cadars, Mohamed Cheikh Abdrabou, Steve Cole, Amy Cordileone, Henry Culpepper, Jeff Culpepper, Keith Cunningham, Tory Davidson, Lucy Davies, Fenella Dawnay, Dominique Delport, Elyse Dodgson, Mike Downey, Emmylou Drys, Sean Egan, Aurélie El Hassak Marzorati, Jack Ellis, Vicky Featherstone, Eric Fellner, Corentin Fila, Annie Gavrilescu, Alan Gartland, Claire Gilbert, Elisa Giovanetti, Patrick Glackin, Laura Griffiths, Sabrina Guinness, Baraa Halabieh, Paul Handley, Andy Harries, Marianna Hay, Raphaël Hilarion, Karthik Iyer, Elizabeth Kesses, Colleen Kollar, Megan Kollar Dwyer, David Lan, Alexander Leff, Brenda Leff, Ottoline Macilwaine, Vincent Mangado, Patricia Moyersoen, Charles Mnene, Carey Mulligan, Anna Murphy, Ruth and Vince Murphy, Sarah Murray, Marie Nore, Rufus Norris, Joanna Ostrom, Laure Pourageaud, Daniel Raggett, Jemma Read, Jenn Reynolds, Ian Rickson, Angela and Mike Robertson, Kate Robertson, Tracey Seaward, Mike Shepherd, Kirstin Shirling, Suzanne Smalley, Chris Sonnex, Juliet Stevenson, Vanessa Stone, Tom Stoppard, Behnam Taheri, Jack Thorne, Mark Tildesley, Kathy Treat, Connie Treves, Claire Verlet, Anne Vickers, Jonathan Vickers, Bruno Wang, Mat Whitecross, Susan Witherow, Lena Zimmer, Zoukak and everyone who has volunteered with us in the UK, France and across the world.

And we extend an enormous thank you to:

All the individuals and organisations whose donations and grants have made it possible for us to build a theatre in Calais and continue Good Chance's work across the world for more than two years. Without you none of this would have been possible.

Good Chance relies on donations, grants and the time and dedication of volunteers. If you would like to support the continued work of the company both in the UK and internationally we would love to hear from you on:

hello@goodchance.org.uk / +44 (0)20 7922 2994

c/o Young Vic, 66 The Cut, London, SE1 8LZ

www.goodchance.org.uk

GoodChanceTheatre

@goodchancecal

goodchancetheatre

Registered charity number 1166833

Company Supporter 2018

PURELAND
FOUNDATION

The Jungle Charity Partner

Help Refugees

The Jungle

Joe Murphy grew up in Leeds and Joe Robertson grew up in Hull. They began writing plays together at university in 2011. Their short plays include *Fairway Manor* (Burton Taylor Studio, Oxford Playhouse), *Ten Bits on Boondoggling* and *Paper Play* (Edinburgh Fringe) and *Maria Popova* (Greater Manchester tram network). In 2015, they established Good Chance Theatre in the 'Jungle' refugee and migrant camp in Calais, a space of expression where theatre, art, dance and music could be made. They lived there for seven months until the eviction of the southern half of the camp. In 2016, Good Chance built its original Calais theatre in view of the UK Parliament for *Encampment*, a major festival at the Southbank Centre in London, with a programme of 110 artists from around the world, run by former residents of the camp. In 2017 Good Chance began working in Paris with theatres, humanitarian organisations and local communities to create new spaces of expression, welcome and introductions. In June 2018, the Good Chance temporary theatres of hope will open again in the north of the city. *The Jungle* is Joe and Joe's first full-length play.

JOE MURPHY
and
JOE ROBERTSON

The Jungle

FABER & FABER

First published in 2017
by Faber and Faber Limited
74–77 Great Russell Street
London WC1B 3DA

This new edition 2018

Typeset by Country Setting, Kingsdown, Kent CT14 8ES
Printed in England by CPI Group (UK) Ltd, Croydon CR0 4YY

A CIP record for this book is available from the British Library

ISBN 978-0-571-35018-6

The Jungle, a co-production between Young Vic and the National Theatre with Good Chance Theatre, commissioned by the National Theatre, opened at the Young Vic on 7 December 2017. The cast, in alphabetical order, was as follows:

Henri/Yasin Raphael Acloque
Amal Aliya Ali, Alyssa Denise D'Souza
Norullah Mohammad Amiri
Muzamil Elham Ehsas
Boxer Trevor Fox
Omid Moein Ghobsheh
Derek Michael Gould
Safi Ammar Haj Ahmad
Mohammed Ansu Kabia
Yohannes Bruk Kumelay
Sam Alex Lawther
Paula Jo McInnes
Okot John Pfumojena
Beth Rachel Redford
Ali Rachid Sabitri
Omar Mohamed Sarrar
Salar Ben Turner
Helene Nahel Tzegai

Direction Stephen Daldry and Justin Martin
Design Miriam Buether
Costume Catherine Kodicek
Light Jon Clark
Sound Paul Arditti
Composer and Musical Direction John Pfumojena
Video Tristan Shepherd

Casting Julia Horan, CDG
Fights Terry King
Voice Jeannette Nelson
Creative Consultant Amy Reade
Assistant Director Nicole Charles
Design Assistant Joana Dias
Video Producer Tamara Moore
Archive Research Belinda Harris

The Jungle, in this revised version, was first presented in the West End at the Playhouse Theatre, London, on 16 June 2018. A National Theatre and Young Vic co-production with Good Chance Theatre presented by Sonia Friedman Productions and Tom Kirdahy, Hunter Arnold, in association with Elizabeth and Ali Ahmet Kocabiyik, Gary and Marcia Nelson, Ushkowitzlatimer Productions, Paula Marie Black, Tulchin Bartner Productions, Michael DeSantis, 1001 Nights Productions, Rupert Gavin, Brenda Leff, Stephanie P. McClelland, Richard Winkler, Jane Cee and Glenn Redbord. The cast was as follows:

Norullah Mohammad Amiri
Boxer Gerard Carey (until 23 June)
    Trevor Fox (from 25 June)
Henri / French Police Officer / CRS Alexander Devrient
    (understudy Safi, Yasin)
Maz Elham Ehsas (understudy Ali)
Omid Moein Ghobsheh
Safi Ammar Haj Ahmad
Sam Alex Lawther (until 11 August)
    Freddie Meredith (from 13 August)
Paula Jo McInnes
Hamid Yasin Moradi
Mohammed Jonathan Nyati
Okot John Pfumojena
Beth Rachel Redford
Derek Dominic Rowan
Ali Rachid Sabitri
Omar Mohamed Sarrar
Yasin Eric Sirakian (understudy Norullah, Sam, Henri)
Salar Ben Turner
Helene Nahel Tzegai

Little Amal Aliya Ali, Lara Alpay, Alyssa De Souza,
    Erin Rushidi

Understudies Tiran Aakel, Alexander Devrient, Elham Ehsas, Cherno Jagne, Kiki Kendrick, Sara Mohonen, Eric Sirakian.

Direction Stephen Daldry and Justin Martin
Design Miriam Buether
Costume Catherine Kodicek
Light Jon Clark
Sound Paul Arditti
Musical Direction / Composition John Pfumojena
Video Duncan McLean and Tristan Shepherd
Casting Julia Horan, CDG
Executive Producer David Lan
Fights Terry King
Dialects Zabarfjad Salam
Voice Jeannette Nelson
Resident Director Jocelyn Cox
Associate Lighting Designer Rob Casey
Design Assistant Joana Dias
Good Chance Creative Consultant Amy Reade
Company Stage Manager Sunita Hinduja
Stage Manager Georgia Bird
Deputy Stage Manager Edwina Allen
Assistant Stage Managers Kenzie Murray, Lauren Ione
Production Manager Lloyd Thomas
Costume Supervisor Scarlet Wallis
Chaperones Eleanor Herdman for Bea & Co.
Sound No. 1 Mary Stone
Sound No. 2 Liv Nagi, Elliot Williams
Video Operator Julie Rocque
Head of Wardrobe Emma Sheppard
Deputy Wardrobe Florence McGlynn
Make-up and SFX Natalia Osipova

Characters

Ali
thirties, Kurdistan

Norullah
fifteen, Afghanistan

Beth
eighteen, UK

Okot
seventeen, Sudan

Boxer
forties, UK

Omar
twenty-five, Sudan

CRS Officer
France

Omid
twenty-one, Iran

Derek
fifties, UK

Paula
fifties, UK

Helene
twenty-eight, Eritrea

Safi
thirty-five, Syria

Henri
twenties, France

Salar
thirty-two, Afghanistan

Little Amal
six, Syria

Sam
eighteen, UK

Maz
twenty, Afghanistan

Yasin
twenty-four, Iraq

Mohammed
thirty-five, Sudan

This is a fictional account,
inspired by the writers' work in the Jungle

THE JUNGLE

For Sonia and Stephen

'The desperate desire of everyone is that this is a temporary stop. A brief, cold and trying moment. But despite the best intentions, the Jungle is beginning to become a place, with churches and theatres and art and restaurants. It is germinating into that collective home. But then, isn't this how all places once began? With refugees stopping at a river, a beach, a crossroads, and saying, we'll just pause here for a bit. Put on the kettle, kill a chicken.'

A.A. Gill

February, 2016.

An emergency meeting of residents and volunteers inside a makeshift Afghan restaurant in the Jungle refugee and migrant camp in Calais, France.

It is late at night, freezing cold. The restaurant is restless and busy. More and more people congregate, meeting, embracing, exchanging. People wait, smoke, talk, sip sweet milky chai. Hot naan bake in an oven and are passed around.

Paula is recording the names and details of residents. Little Amal, a young girl, is always by her side.

Everyone is dirty, exhausted, wide-eyed on energy drinks, emotional, frightened, cold. Deep, rattling coughs punctuate the noise of talk in many languages and multiple generators growling all around.

Everything happens quickly in the Jungle, all at once, everyone on top of each other and always present.

Derek addresses the room.

Derek Right. Can I have everyone's attention, please? I know there have been a lot of rumours going around. People are frightened. I'm going to explain as clearly as I can the facts as we know them. Can you translate that, please?

Mohammed Arabic.

Salar Pashto.

Helene Tigrinya.

Ali Farsi.

Translations.

Paula Salar, I need your information.

Salar Salar Malikzai. Thirty-two years old. I come from Afghanistan. I've been here eleven months.

Derek Another eviction notice was posted this morning. This one gives police the authority to clear all the southern half of the Jungle. That includes the school, the mosques, the churches.

Helene My church!

Derek Most of the shops . . .

Salar The restaurants?

Derek Yes, Salar, it does include the restaurants.

Translations.

Paula Mohammed?

Mohammed Mohammed Abboud. Thirty-five. I'm from Sudan. Been here eleven months.

Derek The Judge has said it must be an expulsion –

Sam 'Expulsion humanitaire' – a soft eviction –

Derek A soft eviction, which means they cannot use bulldozers. We've heard that maybe the police will start doing something tomorrow. So it's likely, if that happens, they will just be asking people to leave.

Omar (*Arabic*) Where the fuck do they want us to go? There's nowhere!

Paula Helene?

Helene Helene Gebrikidane. Twenty-eight. From Eritrea. Been here eleven months.

Mohammed How can this be legal? They cannot evict us in the middle of winter!

Derek They think they can. So this time we're mounting a legal challenge. Sam.

Shouts of protest.

Salar Oh, here he is!

Helene Leave him.

Sam The government claim the notice is legal because it has promised to rehouse everyone in accommodation centres around France.

Salar Your friends? He is a collaborator!

Maz Hadar!

Sam Which would be legal, but they are only providing 1,500 spaces.

Helene This is joke!

Sam Obviously, their estimate is completely wrong.

Salar How can we trust a word you say?

Derek Salar –

Salar No, no, no, this boy is a liar!

Derek Calm, please!

Sam Unless we can prove, prove to the courts there are many, many more people here –.

Salar No more evictions. You promised us!

Sam And clearly they've fucked us.

Salar goes for Sam. He is held back.

Paula The police are lining up out there and we're fighting each other!

Derek (*taking Sam away*) Sam, let's go.

Paula Now. We need accurate population figures. So we are conducting a census. A record of every man, woman and child living in the Jungle today. Age. Country. Time you've been here. I need this information from everyone.

Omar (*Arabic*) What does she want our information for? She's police!

Mohammed She is not asking you to claim asylum in France. She knows you want to get to UK. Trust the lady.

Paula Thank you, Mohammed. This is how we're going to fight. Legally. Peacefully. With facts. Omar.

Omar Omar Sarrah. Twenty-five. Sudan. Seven months.

Mohammed hands out forms.

Mohammed If you run a business. Cafés, shops. Restaurants, Salar –

Sam Volunteers, Mohammed.

Mohammed Volunteers, if you run a kitchen, a distribution point, women and children's centre, anything, fill this in!

Paula Yasin?

Yasin Yasin Abbas. Seventeen. Palestine. Been here since the beginning.

Beth enters, holding a sheet of paper, leading Little Amal by the hand.

Beth Paula, a boy's been killed on the motorway.

Paula's phone rings.

Paula Fucking hell.

Beth I found her wandering around on her own. Is Norullah on your list?

Paula No.

Beth Norullah Abdul.

Paula I know who he is, Beth.

Beth He's fifteen years old, from Afghanistan.

Paula I haven't seen him. (*Answering her phone.*) Yes?

Beth Salar, have you seen Norullah?

Salar Not today.

Paula (*on her phone*) Fuck's sake!

Beth (*leaving*) Where the hell is he?

Paula Alright, I'm coming. Boxer, are you sober?

Boxer All things considered.

Paula Can I trust you with something?

Boxer What am I supposed to say to that?

Paula Yes, Paula. You can.

Boxer Yes, Paula. Course you bloody can.

Paula Look after Amal. (*To Little Amal.*) I'll be back soon, love. Stay with Uncle Boxer.

Boxer Howay, pet.

Paula (*to Boxer*) Don't let her out of your sight. (*Handing the census to Derek.*) Derek, finish this off.

Derek Where are you going?

Paula A boy's been killed on the motorway.

Derek Not again.

Paula (*exiting*) I'm going to identify the body.

Mohammed Salar, how many people come here?

Salar Everyone.

Mohammed What service do you provide?

Salar Have you tasted my chicken livers?

Mohammed Why is your restaurant vital to life in the Jungle?

Salar (*taking a framed review off the wall*) Here. Give them my *Sunday Times* review.

Mohammed We need to do this, Salar.

Salar Jungle finished. We have said it for months. Now it is true.

Somewhere on the fringes of the camp.

Henri (*French*) Sam, let's speak honestly. As friends.

Sam As friends?

Henri There isn't any more you can do here. I know you built houses. I know you helped. Now they will be destroyed and that's difficult for you, I understand.

Sam No more evictions. You promised me.

Henri You can't have thought that this would last for ever. Go home and rest. Be with your family. And then do something great with your life.

Sam The judge will rule in our favour.

Henri Here is the contact of my successor.

Sam You're leaving?

Henri For Paris.

Sam Back to your Civil Service desk.

Henri Back to civilisation. I would be very sad if our relationship were to end this way.

Sam The whole camp hates me. They're calling me a *hadar*. A collaborator. Would this be happening if I hadn't helped you?

Henri Last piece of advice. Don't stay here. It isn't safe.

Sam hand the census to Derek, who addresses the room.

Derek The census is complete! We have the results! 5,497 people live in the Jungle. Of those, 3,455 are in the eviction zone. 445 are children. 305 unaccompanied. Now we know who we are. This eviction is illegal.

Paula Please, please, give me good news.

Derek Court's adjourned.

Sam Their figures are wrong. We have a case.

Derek Who was it?

Pause.

Paula?

They look to Salar.

Paula Salar? Salar. The boy on the motorway. It was Norullah.

Pause.

I'm sorry.

Salar leaves.

Mohammed Maz. Ali.

They leave, as Beth enters.

Beth Where's everyone going? What's going on?

Sam The boy on the motorway . . .

Beth Oh, God . . .

Paula Beth –

Sam I'm so sorry.

Paula Beth, can I have a word?

Beth How do you know?

Sam Paula identified the body.

Beth No, no, no . . .

Paula It was Norullah.

Beth I need to see him.

Paula They're burying him in Angels Corner.

Beth No. They can't bury him in the mud in Calais.

Derek (*to the room*) Sam, everyone, the judge in Lille is giving her verdict! Sam, translate –

He passes his phone to Sam, who translates from French.

Sam She has considered the case carefully . . . She recognises that the *bidonville* represents a risk to public safety . . .

Boxer *Bidon* – what?

Derek Slum.

Sam However, she recognises the significant infrastructure within the *bidonville* . . . *Les lieux de vie*, the places of life . . .

Derek Yes. Come on!

Sam She recognises a difference between their population figures and the ones we provided . . .

Derek The census worked!

Sam She also recognises the growing number of unaccompanied minors . . .

Cheers.

Paula Fuck, yes!

Derek We've done it!

Sam However . . .

Derek However?

Pause.

Paula What?

Sam Has not been convinced that this evidence is sufficient to change her first verdict . . . Consequently . . . she upholds the notice and gives legal authorisation for the eviction to begin.

Paula Yeah, knock it down. Knock it down and never let it happen again. But not like this. Not when they have nowhere to go. Kids will disappear. Mark my word. Hundreds of them. They'll run, or be taken, and we'll never see them again. Mark my word.

Numbed silence.
The body of a boy is carried on, shrouded in white, raised into the air, bathed in light, then buried. A song is sung in Arabic.

Okot enters.

Okot (*Arabic*) Who is it?

Beth Okot!

Okot Is it him?

Ali (*Kurdish*) What are you doing here, son of a bitch? (*English.*) You should be in Dunkirk.

Beth Dunkirk? We had an agreement, you told me he was in the UK!

Ali (*Kurdish*) Fuck off. Omid!

He calls someone on his phone.

Okot You left before he put me in the lorry.

Ali (*Kurdish*) Omid, grab him!

Okot You promised you would look after Norullah.

Beth Okot, come here.

Okot No good man here.

Beth Okot!

Okot runs.
Beth is restrained by Paula.

Paula What have you done?

Mohammed Get out of here, Ali.

Ali leaves.

Salar Oh! Allah, make him, this child, our means of preservation, and make him a source of reward and treasure for us, and make him a pleader for us, and one whose pleading is accepted.

Mohammed You were close to him.

Salar Norullah was like my son.

Mohammed Did he have parents?

Salar His mother in Kabul. He phoned her every week. Told her he was in UK. In London, with his friends. A family had taken him in. He was starting school. He was learning English.

Paula And he was. Here.

Salar He told her he was happy. I will have to tell her he didn't even make it out of France.

Derek Salar, this isn't your fault.

Salar I kept him here.

Everyone leaves. Boxer is left alone with Little Amal.

Boxer (*to Little Amal as he dresses her in warm clothes*) Amal? Y'alright, pet. Now, it's all getting a bit messy round here, so, you and me, we're going to go on an adventure. Has anyone ever told you about England? Because it's a land full of green fields and great, long rivers. Tiny little island out on its own. And because it's so small, everyone has to be kind. They have to get on and make things work. There's parks with slides, big swings. Beautiful, old schools –

Little Amal School.

Boxer Aye, that's right. Teachers who love you. And anywhere you go, any time of day, you're always welcome. And don't let anyone tell you otherwise.

Now let's get this on you. This jacket belongs to a very special girl. She's called Lottie. You'll meet her soon. She's gunna be your big sister. You're gunna love her. And she's gunna love you. But first, you and me are going to play a little game of hide and seek in the back of Paula's van. And you have to be really, really quiet.

And I promise you. You're going to forget all about this fucking place.

If there's one thing I know. I have been a shit dad. But all that's going to change. Now let's get out of here.

Boxer sweeps her up into his arms and exits.
People enter in chaos.

Derek (*handing out rags to protect against tear gas*) The police have arrived heavily armed and wearing body armour. This dehumanises them. They have tear gas. When they shoot, you need to cover your face, but don't wear gas masks, the police consider them weapons. If you're exposed, wash it off with milk or coke, not water. It is our job to re-humanise the situation –

Mohammed (*running in*) They are here! They have bulldozers!

Derek They can't. The Judge said a soft eviction!

Members of the Compagnies Républicaines de Sécurité (CRS) shoot tear gas into the restaurant.

Paula Amal! Amal!

Derek It can't end like this!

Paula Where the fuck is Boxer?

Mohammed We need to get out of here, Salar!

A huge explosion outside. Salar smiles.

Salar No. We resist.

He stands on a table, raises a sign which reads:

WE ARE SEARCHING FOR FREEDOM IN EUROPE BUT WE FIND NONE.

Sam Beth, come on!

Beth I can't.

Sam We have to go now!

A CRS Officer enters in full riot gear.

CRS Officer *Bouge toi! Bouge toi!*

Beth I won't move.

CRS Officer Don't understand you, girl.

Beth I'm not leaving him here, I can't leave, I'll never leave.

CRS Officer You are in France, you speak French!

Beth stands and faces him.

Beth Look at yourself! This is not France!

The Officer aims a pepper spray canister into her eyes. Safi steps calmly into the pandemonium.

Safi Stop. Let's stop for a moment.

TWO
THE BIRTH

In peace and quiet, he addresses everyone.

Safi They warned us in Libya. The smugglers. They advised us about safe passage. How to stay hidden, avoid arrest. And one thing they say to me, again and again, I remember . . .

He speaks the quotation in Arabic, then in English.

'Beware the French. They have absolutely no manners.'

My name is Safi Al-Hussain. Thirty-five years young. Former student of English Literature and Language in my home town, Aleppo. So I know a little bit about telling stories. Always start at the end.

Another quotation for you. 'If you open me up when I am dead you will find Calais engraved upon my heart.' One of your queens said that. Is it true for you? Maybe because your armies fought over Calais for so many centuries, which is bizarre to me. Have you ever been there? Or maybe, if you like history, it is because you know that Julius Caesar invaded you from Calais in 54 BC. Or maybe the other BC? Booze cruise . . .?

Open me up. You'll find it there. Engraved upon my heart. Like many before me, I lived there to get here. And it takes pain to live side by side. If you are born in the same country as another person this is true. If you are born in a different country, a different continent, even more. Some people will tell you living together is easy, but you mustn't trust them. These are difficult things, my friends. I do not pretend we did not make mistakes. And many more will be made in the telling of this story, I am sure. We started at the end, so let's go back to the beginning.

March 2015 is the date of birth.

Salar and Mohammed meet. They are cleaner, more awake, looking years younger.

Mohammed What a dump.

Safi Mohammed Abboud, former Professor at the University of Khartoum.

Mohammed This is the worst place in Europe.

Salar Tonight we will be free.

Mohammed If we live that long.

Salar They said the land is ours to use. We can build here.

Safi Salar Malikzai. A restaurant owner from Karz, near Kandahar.

More people enter, carrying bags, tents and sleeping bags.

Mohammed Let's count the things that kill us. Chemicals. Snakes. The filthy land, all rubbish.

Salar Better than bombs, Mohammed.

Mohammed Cold, wind, rain –

Salar Terrorists, the Taliban –

Mohammed The French police!

Salar Drought, famine –

Mohammed Each other?

Salar We are safer than at any time in our lives.

Mohammed There are tensions between our people. Before, we lived in separate places. There was no problem. Now we must live together.

Salar So we live apart.

Mohammed There is no space to live apart.

Salar Look around, my friend. It's already done.

They divide the land.

Ali Here! Here we build Kurdistan.

Yasin Here! Here is Palestine.

Omid This! This is Iran.

Helene This! This is Eritrea.

Safi This! This is Syria.

Salar And this is Afghanistan. Sudan?

Mohammed If this is going to work, you and I must stand together.

Salar We will, my friend. We will.

Mohammed This, this will be Sudan . . .

Safi We were forced from many places into one. And this place we called –

Salar Zhangal!

A drumbeat begins.

Safi A Pashto word, which means forest. But this was no forest. It was an old landfill site on the edge of

Calais. A *zone tolerée* to solve the crisis of migrant squats inside the city, generously located only a short walk to the ferry port. Everyone tries. You know this word, a good word all languages understand. Try is the reason we are here. Try for train. Try for boat. Try for UK. The first nights it is like the sea is in two parts and we walk to UK on a simple path. So many try. So many succeed!

People try to cross the border.

All Yayayayayayaya!

Safi The sound we make when someone arrives safely to UK. We call this good chance. Good chance is the dream.

Norullah No chance!

Safi Police at port! So we go for the trains instead.

Norullah No chance!

Safi Police at train! So we go back for the port.

Norullah Dugar! Dugar! Dugar!

Safi Dugar is a miracle. Dugar is why we sing. Dugar means traffic jam. When lorries begin to slow and horns are loud, we see our dreams may happen.

All Yayayayayayaya!

Safi We call it the game! We are young men. Strong, brave. We climb fences, jump lorries, escape police. And, if I can say, the game is fun. Yes, sometimes they catch us. But French police are strange. They let you go every time, to try and try again! Go back to Zhangal!

All No chance!

Safi This was night. And in the day, we built.

Building begins all around.

Look around at the squalor, people shitting, burning plastic, asbestos in the sand, wet clothes with no chance to dry. We built because we had to. Everywhere, the sound of saws, hammers, work. In the absence of any help from the French state, we did it ourselves.

Henri (*French*) No, no, no. We built a centre. Le Centre de Jules Ferry. With sleeping places for women and children. Showers.

People are confused. The drumming stops.

Safi Monsieur. No one here speaks French.

Henri No one? Ah, *merde*. (*He stumbles into English.*) We have built . . . a compound. It has sleeping places for women and the children –

Safi But most of us are men.

Henri We will give one meal day, for everyone. And ten warm showers.

Safi For eight thousand people?

Henri Funded by the generosity of France.

Norullah Fuck France!

Henri (*exiting*) Of course. Bon chance.

Safi There are hundreds arriving every day!

The call to prayer sounds.

This was five times a day at home. Now we hear it from mosques in Zhangal. It means, come to pray. Come to success. At home, they were fighting. In Zhangal, they were praying, Sunni and Shia together.

Helene sings 'Lord Have Mercy'.

Christians, too. The church of St Michael, protector and leader of army of God. With a makeshift steeple, six metres high. Images of the Virgin and Winnie the Pooh. The church of your imagination.

Helene Everyone is welcome to bask in the glory of the Lord!

Safi Beautiful words.

Helene They are a gift from God, like my journey.

Safi How far did you come?

Helene I walk from Eritrea to Sudan.

Safi That's a thousand miles.

Helene From Sudan to Libya.

Safi Two thousand miles, across open desert.

Helene After twenty-seven days, I reach the Mediterranean in Tripoli, and lose all hope. Until God showed me a sign.

Safi Did He walk on water?

Helene No, real sign, for travel agent. 'Cruises to Lampedusa. No visa required.' Praise be to God.

Safi Did God pay the travel agent, too?

Helene No, but He got me good discount.

Helene resumes singing as she exits.

Safi You know this song? Maybe you learnt it in school. Lord Have Mercy. In Tigrinya.

Yasin (*to Ali, in Arabic*) Help me. Can you get me across the border?

Ali What?

Safi Speak English.

Yasin I lie three days, three nights behind fence at station. No food, no water. Rain so cold. France police beat me. I cannot stay here.

Ali This is bad place.

Yasin You can help me.

Ali What kind of help are you looking for?

Yasin You know.

Everyone looks at Ali.

Ali You want help to get to UK too, my friends? (*Handing out business cards, then addressing Safi.*) Syrian? We should talk.

Safi You think my bones are made of gold?

Ali I'm sure we can make a deal. Ali. Call me. (*To Yasin.*) Come.

Yasin follows Ali off.

Safi More people means more opportunities. Smugglers. A marketplace. And one day, a new idea.

Safi is nearly knocked over by Norullah on a bike overfilled with Lidl bags, which spill all over the floor.

Safi You OK, my friend?

Norullah Fucking dick bike!

Safi Where's all this from?

Norullah Lidl.

Safi Lidl? A Pashto word?

Norullah Fucking shop.

Safi This is a lot of food. Is it all for you?

Norullah I sell.

Safi And people buy?

Norullah If I sell, people buy.

Salar Bambino! Quick!

Safi Clever boy.

Norullah scrambles to pick up the bags and runs to Salar, who sends him back to retrieve the ones he has left.

Salar If we do this, we do it properly. You understand?

He gives Norullah a wad of money.

Norullah I'm not bambino.

Salar Norullah, my man. My restaurant man.

They begin to build a restaurant.
Okot enters and rifles through Norullah's bags for food.

Safi A restaurant. Mosques, churches, shops. And people from many countries living together in peace –

Norullah spots Okot and sprints towards him. A fight breaks out.

Norullah What the fuck! Fucking black man, fucking thief!

Okot I was only looking! Crazy fucking Afghan!

Mohammed and Salar separate them.

Norullah All you fucking black man same. Big problem!

Safi Problem. Another word. More people means more problems.

After consulting Okot and Norullah, Salar and Mohammed meet where the boys were. It could be

32

a standoff, but the situation settles. The two boys remain, facing each other.

Mohammed The Galloo Squat has just been evicted. Three hundred people are waiting under the bridge.

Salar What are they waiting for?

Mohammed There aren't enough tents!

Helene People are sleeping in my church.

Salar Why is she in my restaurant?

Helene She is called Helene.

Salar You should be in the French centre. There are sleeping places for women there.

Safi The centre only has a few places. It was full after a week.

Salar Where is her husband?

Helene I do not have husband.

Salar Zhangal is no place for woman on her own.

Helene And that is why I am here. Our voices should be heard at these meetings.

Salar Meeting? This is not a meeting.

Helene Every new arrival means one less tent for Eritrean women.

Salar After good chance tonight, there will be tents tomorrow.

Mohammed And then more people again.

Safi Eight thousand landed on Lesvos yesterday.

Salar How do you know this?

Safi The Facebook and Whatsapp groups say it. The same number crossed to Macedonia over the weekend. The Balkans route is full.

Salar They go to Germany.

Ali Not all. Many are coming here.

Salar Why is he in my restaurant?

Safi Ali speaks for the Kurdish people. Mohammed, Sudan. Helene, Eritrea. And I speak for Syria.

Salar Speak for?

Ali Doesn't look like a restaurant to me.

Salar It's not finished.

Ali I'll make sure I come back when it is.

Salar No smugglers allowed.

Mohammed Gentlemen. We need to talk about violence, not make more. We have a duty.

Salar Duty to who?

Mohammed Our people.

Salar Our people? To make the sun shine? To make the rain stop? To open the border?

Safi To meet together. Representatives of all the camp's nationalities.

Salar What problems?

Helene Toilets.

Salar Tell your people to shit properly.

Helene It is difficult with so much infection.

Salar So they should wash properly!

Ali Police violence.

Salar It is their job. It is the same everywhere.

Mohammed Fighting.

34

Salar The Sudanese are thieves.

Mohammed Afghans are racist.

Salar If a black man steals, can we not say?

Helene Always, always problem!

Mohammed Our young boys, Salar. I promise you, it is not long before someone is killed.

Safi We need to act before it gets out of control.

Pause.

Salar How?

Safi We ask our Imams to talk about peace in their khutbas tomorrow.

Salar We needed a meeting to decide this?

Mohammed Yes. People need leaders. And we should walk through the camp together, speak to everyone, hand in hand.

Salar Mohammed. I am not an elder.

Mohammed But you are respected. Afghanistan is one of the largest communities –

Salar The largest, *the* . . .

Safi Without you there is no hope, Salar.

Ali We could hold future meetings here in your restaurant!

Salar Future meetings?

Ali It will be good for business.

Safi What do you think, Salar?

Pause.

Salar OK. No problem. (*Pashto.*) Norullah, come here. Shake his hand.

Norullah (*Pashto*) I'm not touching him.

Salar (*Pashto*) You do what I say. (*English.*) Shake his hand.

Norullah steps towards Okot.

Mohammed (*to Okot*) Go to him. Shake his hand. (*Arabic.*) Go!

They shake hands.

Salar No more fighting. We are hated by enough people.

Mohammed Thank you, Salar.

Salar (*to Helene*) You are very welcome.

Salar exits.

Safi It is August. We have been in Zhangal five months. More and more people arrive, making journeys across the terrible sea. Walking through Europe, like we did, to safety, to our dreams.

Omid plays the guitar and sings.

Safi People meet, sing, share stories of great journeys, stories of home.

Ali Safi, I have place in lorry tonight.

Safi I think I'll stay.

Ali (*Arabic*) Are you mad?

Safi For now.

Ali Find me when you come to your senses.

Safi Thanks, Ali.

Ali You have an open ticket, remember. Call me.

Safi Yes, Zhangal is unclean. Yes, it smells. Yes, nowhere to shit. Sometimes good chance, sometimes no chance.

Yes, little food, water, space, tents, clothes. Yes, you see children play in European mud.

Omid sings louder.

But more. More hope than you have seen in all lifetimes. More people of heart and song than you have ever heard. This is Omid, from Isfahan. He carried this guitar all the way from Iran. He played it for police at the Serbian border. They told him, 'If you're any good, we'll let you pass.' This song gave him and two hundred others safe passage.

Omar starts to play the drums.

And this is Omar, from Dbebah in Sudan. He's written a song with his friend Khalid about French police in Calais.

When you do not have enough of anything, you make from nothing.

The Afghan national anthem is sung riotously by Maz, Norullah and Salar.

Salar The Afghan flag! An Afghan restaurant. Serving traditional Afghan food. My restaurant is open!

Norullah My restaurant!

A celebration, driven by tiredness and squalor, ignites. Salar, supported by Norullah and Maz, serves the first meals. TVs blast out Bollywood movies as music from all nationalities collides into one.

Beth enters, holding her phone, which displays the photograph of Alan Kurdi.

Silence.

Safi Then, in September, everything changed.

THREE
THE ARRIVAL

Beth A photograph of a boy . . . A little boy in blue shorts and a red top . . . Washed up on a beach . . .

She shows everyone the photo.

Safi Alan. Alan Kurdi. From Kobani in northern Syria. (*To Beth.*) Are you OK?

Beth I just . . . I saw this . . . and . . . I thought I should –

Safi Norullah!

Norullah goes to her, stuffs a fresh naan bread into her hands.

Norullah This is the best bread in the whole of France!

Beth Thank you . . .

Norullah You are UK. You have good seat.

Beth I don't need –

Norullah Sit. You queen. I am Norullah.

Beth Hello, Norullah. I'm Beth.

Norullah Miss Beth. I am one five.

Beth One five? Oh, fifteen. I am one eight.

Norullah But I am not bambino. I am restaurant man.

Beth It's a beautiful restaurant.

Norullah English no good. I from Kabul.

Beth Afghanistan?

Norullah You know?

Beth I haven't been, but –

38

Norullah Afghanistan best country in world. Except one. You know!

Beth Do I?

Norullah finds this hysterical.

Norullah (*to Safi, in Pashto*) You think she will take me to UK?

Safi (*Pashto*) I don't know. Ask her.

Norullah (*Pashto*) You ask her!

Safi Norullah would like to ask you a question.

Beth Oh, OK.

Norullah You . . .

He mimes a car.

Beth Yes, I have a car.

Norullah Me, small. I . . . (*To Safi, in Pashto.*) I could hide in the back.

Safi He says he could hide in the back.

Beth I don't understand.

Safi And then you could drive him to UK.

Beth Oh . . .

Norullah Please.

Beth No, I'm sorry, Norullah. I can't do that.

Norullah Why?

Beth How can I explain this? Car is bad. Police look inside. Police arrest me. Do you understand?

Safi Sorry, my friend. She says no.

Norullah Big problem!

Safi We spend months trying to get to UK. And in September, UK came here.

Paula enters with bags of donations.

Paula I've got a thousand tents in the back of a truck.

Paula drops the tents at her feet.

Hamid Line! Line! Line!

Paula Anyone? Who the fuck's in charge here?

She sees Little Amal.

Fuck me, she's a baby. (*To Safi.*) Where's her mum and dad?

Safi Not here.

Paula Go and get them. She shouldn't be running around in the mud on her own.

Safi I mean they're not in France.

Paula This isn't France, it's a fucking joke. Where's the UN?

Safi They have to be invited.

Paula Save the Children?

Safi Haven't seen them.

Paula Fucking Red Cross?

Safi Who?

Paula Have you called them?

Safi Me? I'm a refugee.

Paula (*going to Little Amal*) Hello, love. She's fucking soaking. Feel this,

Safi It's raining.

Paula (*leaving, taking Little Amal with her*) Come on, darling. Let's find you something warm to wear.

Derek enters.

Derek On behalf of my country, I am so sorry.

Mohammed You don't have to apologise.

Derek It's a shame on us. We should be ashamed. But what you're building here . . . How is it organised?

Safi People work together. Community leaders meet to discuss problems. This is Mohammed from Sudan.

Derek Incredible.

Mohammed And the problems are great.

Derek This is a city.

Mohammed I have not heard this word about Zhangal before.

Derek What did you call it?

Mohammed Zhangal.

Derek What's he saying?

Safi Zhangal. A Pashto word that means –

Derek Jungle!

Safi Not quite.

Derek 'Now this is the law of the Jungle, and the Law runneth forward and back,
   'The strength of the Pack is the Wolf, and the strength of the Wolf is the Pack.'

Mohammed You must be very tired.

Derek Although short, the journey has been long. I feel I've been on a path here my entire life.

Sam enters, filming everything with his phone.

Sam (*narrating*) I'm standing inside the Jungle refugee and migrant camp in Calais, France. It's obviously a humanitarian crisis. Less than an hour on the Eurostar from St Pancras. It's a big area, sand dunes, along an embankment up to the motorway. I can see the paths that migrants use to get to the lorries. Must be less than a mile to the port. Lots of fences, more fences being built. Maybe five or six thousand tents, some makeshift shacks. One police officer standing on the bridge watching over the camp. He doesn't seem to be doing anything. I was expecting more authority. But there don't seem to be any checkpoints at all. (*To Yasin.*) Oh, hello. Where are you from? Photo?

Yasin (*snatching Sam's phone*) No photos!

The phone is instantly traded, and traded again. Suddenly lots of people are involved.

Sam I'm sorry. If I could just have my phone back, please, I'll delete it.

Maz No speak English.

Sam My phone? Phone?

Safi Norullah! (*Pashto.*) Give him his phone.

Norullah gives it to Sam.

Sam Thank you.

Safi Ask before you take someone's photo, OK?

Beth (*to Sam*) Are you alright? I'm Beth.

Sam Hey! I'm Sam. What the fuck?

Beth I know, right.

Sam Insane

Beth It's like –

Sam Glastonbury. Without the toilets.

Beth Yeah.

Sam How long have you –

Beth Four days.

Sam It's incredible.

Beth The stories –

Sam What are you going to do?

Beth Do?

Sam I'm thinking about housing. There are big opportunities here.

Derek I'll put you in touch with Help Refugees. They're a young grassroots organisation working with Medicin Sans Frontières on a new shelter model. I'm Derek.

Sam That'd be great. Sam.

Beth Housing is a really good idea. I mean, it's sort of OK now, but –

All Winter.

Beth *and* **Derek** With the wind.

All From the sea.

Sam I know.

Derek Things are going to get really awful here. People need to organise, politically.

Paula enters with Little Amal, who is wearing dry new clothes.

Paula Tell me you're from a major NGO.

Derek No, sorry, I'm from Reading.

Paula Halle-fucking-lujah. Paula.

Derek Derek.

Sam Sam.

Beth Beth.

Norullah (*entering, clutching a cup of tea for Beth*) Norullah. Best tea in the whole of France.

Beth I'm going to build a school.

Sam Great idea.

Beth I think it's the first idea I've ever had.

Boxer enters with Helene, playing his banjo and duetting 'I Wanna Be Like You' from The Jungle Book. *Helene pushes him away, and he finds the other volunteers.*

Boxer *Salam aleykum!* Tell you what, those Eritreans know how to put it away! One euro for a can of Petroburg? Pints haven't been this cheap since Kevin Keegan was playing for Newcastle! Boxer, Boxer, Boxer, Boxer. Nice to meet you, nice to meet you. Lots of newbies here, then. I've been here since last Monday. Hitched a ride down from Toon. Snuck on a ferry! Get out, get lost, find this. Half an hour, I'm chilling with a group of Pakistanis, a blind Mexican, some Afghan squidge and I'm banging on me banjo.

Paula Jesus Christ.

Norullah No. Boxer.

Boxer I've said that, keep up. Like the workhorse. I'm here to fix stuff. Anything designed before 1890. After that it gets a bit complimicated. I've got a theory, right. Everyone here is running from something. We're all refugees. So the game is –

44

Norullah What you running from!

Boxer I'll gan first. Missus is a dragon. Custody of the bairn. Always will have because she's a fucking lawyer, fucking minted. Dragging me o'er coals for child support. Doesn't let me see her. And I bloody love that girl, my Lottie. So that's why I'm here. Fleeing the authoritarian regime of my ex-wife. And what does that make me?

Norullah Refugee!

Boxer There we go, the little comrade. (*To Derek.*) How's about this one?

Derek Boxer, we were just speaking about –

Boxer No, come on, Worzel Gummidge. What you running away from, matey?

Derek I don't feel I am running away. I'm running towards.

Boxer Ah, towards what?

Derek Community. I've found things here that have all but disappeared in Britain.

Boxer whispers to Norullah.

Norullah Not happy at home?

Derek I think we'd all agree our country has changed. People don't talk to each other.

Boxer *and* **Norullah** Refugee!

Boxer (*to Beth*) What about you, little miss? Shouldn't you be in school?

Beth I've finished actually.

Boxer Haven't got a job? Uni?

Beth One day, maybe.

Boxer What's wrong with uni?

Beth Three years of my life. Seventy grand of debt. For what? I just felt everything was sort of shit.

Boxer (*to Norullah*) What do you reckon?

Norullah Refugee!

Boxer What about you, bonny lad?

Sam It's terribly important to be able to see and understand different cultures. Bear witness.

Boxer Jesus, say no more! Put that silver spoon back in your mouth, Paddington Bear Witness! You'll have someone's eye out.

Boxer *and* **Norullah** Refugee!

Boxer (*to Paula*) Thou, my darling?

Paula Getting away from wankers like you.

Norullah absolutely pisses himself.

Boxer Orf, kinky.

Norullah Kinky?

Boxer We'll come back to that. (*To Safi.*) What about you, mate?

Safi Me?

Norullah The civil war in Syria.

Boxer Yeah, that'd do it. Refugee.

The volunteers are alone in the centre, the residents looking at them. There is a strange, brief moment. 'Us' and 'them'.
 Salar walks into the centre, rips Boxer's can of beer away.

Salar Everybody out!

Boxer Oy!

Salar Now! (*To Boxer.*) No drinking in my restaurant. I've told you before!

Everyone leaves, apart from the elders.

Salar Now there is a problem. The British.

Helene They are so funny.

Mohammed What about them?

Salar What are they doing here?

Helene They want to help.

Salar Why?

Mohammed 'None of you will be a believer until he loves for his brother what he loves for himself.'

Salar You use the Prophet's words? They are not believers!

Helene They follow Jesus Christ. Do for others like you want them to do for you.

Salar They do not follow Christ. I've seen more of them in your nightclub than in your church.

Helene They might not be Christian, but at least they can dance.

Salar We're not here to dance. And we don't need help.

Helene It's nice to afford food from restaurant. Eritreans have nothing.

Salar Hunger is good. It gets us to UK.

Ali A funny idea for the restaurant man.

Salar I suppose you like them.

Ali Actually I agree with you. We don't need them.

Salar Thank you.

Ali But we may want them. Have your boy count your takings. Then say you don't want them.

Salar Have you forgotten why we're here? We eat for UK, sleep for UK, shit for UK. We need quiet for this, and darkness. Our people think the British will help them get to UK. They won't. They don't care about that.

Helene I spoke with a woman who says people in UK don't know what is happening here.

Salar You believe this?

Helene If they know, maybe the border will open.

Salar They know.

Mohammed This is a good chance for us. A lady wants to build a library. There are plans for a school. Real wooden houses.

Salar I have heard there may be a theatre for entertainment.

Mohammed All of these things are important.

Salar Important for who?

Salar notices Norullah leaving.

(*Pashto.*) Where are you going?

Norullah Miss Beth, school.

Salar absorbs this. He takes Norullah, stands him on the table in front of everyone.

Salar This boy is a refugee. He is a warrior. His father was killed by the Taliban. He walked here. He builds this place with me. He buys food from the shop every day. He provides for all the people of Zhangal. He does not need a school. He needs UK. And they need boys like him. He will work. He will prosper. He will build and buy and sell, and he will provide for all the people there. He does not need UK in Zhangal. He needs UK in UK. And Inshallah, he will get it.

All Inshallah.

Helene So what are you saying, Salar? We kick them out?

Salar Yes.

Helene How do we do this?

Salar We tell them, go! You are not wanted.

All You are not the border man, Salar.

Helene Salar deports from Zhangal!

Mohammed When I arrive in UK, I hope for welcome. Now we should offer them the same.

Safi We must come to a decision about this. A vote.

Salar Vote?

Safi Everyone can give their mind.

Salar We do not vote. We agree.

Ali Agree with you?

Salar Yes.

Mohammed No, this is a good idea. There is disagreement, so we vote.

Safi Do we accept help of British man. Do we welcome him. Who says yes?

Helene, Ali and Mohammed raise their hands.
Norullah does too, and Salar chastises him.

Safi Salar?

Salar I know what British are like. They go to places they don't belong and tell people what to do. They have done so in Afghanistan many times. Not here. Not in Zhangal.

Helene Jungle, they call it.

Salar Jungle? So already they make us animals. If they stay, they support us in everything. They do not tell us what to do, Safi. They do not decide.

Safi First they stayed one night. Then they stayed two nights. Then, they moved in!

FOUR
THE GOLD RUSH

Derek opens the first full meeting of the people of the Jungle.

Derek Welcome! Salam! Darood! To the first democratic meeting in the history of the Jungle! I am Derek. I have come from the UK to stand in solidarity with you.

Chants of 'UK' drown Derek out. He waits until they subside. Translations throughout the room.

Safi and I will chair these meetings, and our first agenda has grown into quite the formidable document. We have distribution, education, housing –

Norullah Place for shit!

Derek Yes, sanitation is on here. Police violence, wifi, green energy . . .

Yasin UK! Wanna talk about UK!

Maz (*singing*) Glory, glory Man United! Glory, glory Man United!

Derek This is a safe space!

All Glory, glory Man United! And fuck you, Arsenal!

Derek OK, perhaps we can save our feelings about Arsenal for any other business? First, I want to kick off with a thought I've been having. The name of this place, our temporary home. It does not feel like a jungle to me.

Maz Jungle for animal, not human!

Derek Yes, it's a town. A thriving, bubbling town. A town of hope. So I want to propose we change it. A new name.

Cheers.

A more fitting name!

Louder cheers.

Hope Town!

Silence.

Let's put that on the agenda for next time. Paula.

Salar No, I will speak. I would like to say thank you to British man for coming here. Already you have been great help. Now is like gold rush in the Jungle. And I know it can be difficult to treat all nationalities equally. But I know you will find ways of being fair, and of maintaining peace in Zhangal. Thank you, British man.

Pause.

Derek OK. Paula.

Paula Women and Children's Centre. Thank you, Boxer, for the building.

Boxer Not blown down yet!

Paula Women's distribution on Monday. Kids on Wednesday. And I know we're all on our fucking high

51

horses here, but send the kids to me. No one else is looking after them. Fuck knows where Save the Children are –

Norullah (*pointing at his nose*) Fuck nose!

Paula Certainly not saving the fucking children.

Norullah (*pointing at himself*) Fucking children!

Paula Dublin III. Remember that name. It's an EU law which gives all unaccompanied children who have family in Europe the right to be reunited with them. Legally. In a Eurostar, not on top of one. Trouble is, our Home Secretary, Theresa darling buds of fucking May, doesn't give a shit. So we're taking her to court. And we will win. If you see a child on their own, send them to the centre. We will get them to safety. And darling little Norullah, give me my fucking phone back. End of speech.

She leaves to applause from residents of the camp.

Derek Right, next on the agenda: Beth's school.

Beth's school.
An English lesson is happening. Everyone is on their feet acting out a story together, their story, about trying to get to the UK.

Beth OK, English this morning. Tenses. Let's go back to the present. Tell me about the lorries!

Norullah We climb on top of lorry roof, then cut.

Beth What with?

Norullah Have knife.

Maz I have knife!

Everyone in the class pulls out a knife.

Beth Knives in pockets, please.

Norullah This word, the thing we cut?

Beth The canvas?

Norullah Canvas. Then climb to hole.

Beth Climb through the hole.

Norullah Yes! Sorry. Climb through the hole. Then take from shoes.

Beth Take what from shoes?

Helene The strings!

Beth The laces? Why?

Norullah For tie up hole!

Yasin To stop the light come in when police have search.

Beth Have you all done this?

All Yes!

Beth God. What happens next?

Omar We hide.

Beth Where?

Norullah Box.

Beth In the box?

Norullah We hide inside the box. Box farest from the lorry door.

Beth *Furthest* from the lorry door.

Norullah Oh, shit! Yes, good. *Furthest* from the lorry door.

Beth Why the furthest?

Norullah So police don't find!

Beth Good. You hide yourself inside the box *furthest* from the lorry door.

Norullah No!

Beth Go on . . .

Norullah My friend from Afghanistan –

Maz Hello! I am friend!

Norullah He . . .

Yasin He hided you.

Beth He hid you. It's an . . .

All Exception!

Beth Hid is the past tense, but we're still in the present. So . . .

Norullah So, he hides me . . .

Beth Because?

Norullah Because I can't hide myself!

Beth Very good! All together now, back to the beginning. You climb on top of the lorry roof.

Norullah I cut the canvas with my knife –

Omar I climb through hole –

Yasin I tie the hole with shoe laces –

Maz And my friend from Afghanistan –

Helene Hides me inside a box –

Maz Box furthest from the lorry door –

Norullah Because I can't hide myself!

Beth Now we're getting somewhere! Write that down.

Everyone writes this down in their exercise books.

Norullah (*to Little Amal*) Little shit, give me pencil!

Little Amal runs to him with a pencil.

Sam (*to Beth*) Sorry to interrupt but do you always teach in those leggings?

Beth I'm sorry, what's wrong with my leggings?

Sam Nothing. Just that some of the other female volunteers cover their arms, legs. Saw a girl from Chiswick basically arrive in a burka.

Beth I don't really think about it, to be honest. But I'm glad you are. Thanks.

Sam I'm not having a go.

Beth No, I know.

Sam Just interested.

Beth I'm glad you see me as a female volunteer.

Sam Not just that.

Beth While we're on clothing, you should ditch the Barbour jacket. This isn't *Monarch of the Glen*.

She turns back to the class.

OK, what next?

Norullah My friend closes the door.

Beth What door? I thought you came in through a hole?

Norullah This is different try. We try five times each night.

Helene Keep up, Beth!

Beth Sorry! So your friend closes the door.

Norullah Not my friend. My friend –

Maz Hello!

Norullah He is inside the lorry

Maz I am inside the lorry.

Helene Everyone knows you can't lock lorry door from inside lorry.

Maz I think Miss Beth has never try!

Norullah You should try, Miss Beth!

All Miss Beth! Miss Beth! Miss Beth!

Safi enters with Okot.

Norullah (*putting a jacket on Beth*) Don't forget your coat!

Maz Journey is going to be very cold!

Beth Please tell me this lorry isn't refrigerated.

Norullah Fridge lorry best lorry because police don't think you stupid enough to try.

Maz Fridge lorry worst lorry because maybe you die.

Norullah Best lorry.

Maz And worst lorry.

Beth Seriously, please don't get in a refrigerated lorry, OK? Who closes the door?

Norullah Man!

Omar Hello!

Beth Do you pay the man?

Norullah No, no. No money for smuggler. He is helped me.

Beth He what? Present tense.

Norullah He is helping me.

Beth Complete the sentence.

Norullah He is helping me hide inside the lorry!

Safi Beth, I have a new student for you.

Beth jumps out of the box and goes to greet Okot. Norullah eyes him.

Beth Great! What's your name?

Okot doesn't respond.

Safi He's called Okot. He's from Darfur.

Norullah Big problem!

Beth Well, it's nice to meet you, Okot. We're learning English today, by telling a story. So, we've cut the canvas of a non-refrigerated lorry, climbed through the hole, hidden inside a box, and that's where we are at the moment.

Safi He doesn't want to stay for long.

Beth That's OK. What happens next, Norullah?

They whisper the following lines.

Norullah Lorry drive. Is drive long way. I think this is good chance!

Yasin Then lorry stops.

Norullah I hear the door.

Maz Torch shines in.

Omar Box lid opens.

Beth Oh, no! Who is it?

Helene Police!

Norullah But special police. He look at me and smiles . . .

Beth What do you think happens next, Okot?

Okot I don't understand.

Beth What does the policeman say?

Okot He says, go back to Jungle, no chance.

Norullah He said, fuck you!

Beth Norullah, no. Okot is our policeman. What happens next. This time, past tense.

Norullah Oh, shit. D, d, d . . .

Beth You can do it.

Norullah Same night –

Beth The same night –

Norullah Shit, the same night, I got in different lorry. But this time I use my mind.

Okot Used. It's used.

Norullah Fucking D! Used! I can't do fucking past!

Beth The past is hard, but you can do it.

Helene Everyone goes for the furthest box.

Norullah But I went for the nearest. Then lorry drived –

Okot Drove. It's drove.

Beth Good, Okot! It's an –

All Exception!

Norullah Mother fucking exception!

58

Norullah goes for Okot and they fly into a brawl.
Beth tries to separate them but is hit by a stray hand.
Yasin tries to break them up, but the fight continues
until Safi pulls the two boys apart.

Safi Everyone out!

Norullah (*exiting*) Your sister give me blowjob!

The school empties.
Beth, Okot and Safi are left alone. Okot has a cut
across his head.

Beth Shit . . .

Safi Are you alright?

Beth I'm fine.

Safi We fight, we fought, we will fight . . .

Safi gives her a first-aid box.

Beth Right, Okot, let's get you cleaned up. How long
have you been here?

He doesn't respond.

Safi Two months.

Beth Your age?

Safi He says he's twenty.

Beth Your real age?

Okot Seventeen.

Beth Are you here by yourself?

Okot My uncle has good chance. He is in Leicester.

Beth Does everyone have an uncle in Leicester? This will
hurt.

As she cleans the cut on his forehead, Beth notices scars and bruises down his neck.

Beth Have you been trying every night? Your neck is . . .

Okot This is from long time. Not from trying.

Beth Have you thought about claiming asylum here?

Okot Why would I do this?

Beth France is a good country.

Okot You think this is a good country?

Beth The Jungle isn't France. There are loads of great cities.

Okot I have one dream only. To stand on white cliffs of Dover and see Jungle this big . . . .

Beth Inshallah.

Okot (*impressed*) Inshallah.

Beth Your English is really good.

Okot My mother taught me. She always tells me words are important. I learn for her.

Beth *From* her.

Okot No. *For* her.

Beth looks to Safi for guidance.

Safi He wants your phone number. It's up to you.

She hands Okot her phone. He types in his number then calls his own phone. The ringtone is 'There'll be Bluebirds Over the White Cliffs of Dover'. He hands the phone back and goes to leave.

Beth Come back tomorrow?

Okot God willing, tonight I have good chance. I call you tomorrow from Leicester. Just you wait and see . . .

Safi He's a good boy.

Sam enters with a large map of the Jungle, separated into numbered sections, or 'quadrants'.

Sam What do you think?

Beth I don't know . . .

Sam It's a map of the Jungle. My housing distribution methodology.

Beth What's number four?

Sam Quadrant four. South, along Route des Gravelines.

Beth Kurdistan?

Sam No, it's an area where some Kurdish people live.

Beth Otherwise known as Kurdistan.

Sam But where does Kurdistan end and Iran begin?

Beth Sounds like Kurdistan to me.

Sam It's imprecise.

Beth The world's imprecise.

Sam I have divided my map into quadrants. The area of the Jungle where lots of Kurdish people live, which is also an area where some Iranians live, as well as some Pakistanis, Palestinians and several caravans of people from Peckham, that is quadrant four.

Beth With its unique and ancient culture.

Sam If we call it Kurdistan it creates tensions. It has to be objective.

Everyone enters.

Derek Sam has been working hard on a system for housing distribution.

Sam I'm going to explain my methodology for distributing houses. I have considered many factors, of which nationality is only one. Above all, we must be fair.

Ali Where is Kurdistan?

Sam It isn't on there.

Ali You don't recognise State of Kurdistan?

Sam No. I mean, yes. I'm grouping it in this quadrant here with Iraq and Iran –

Ali You're doing what?

Sam Or not.

Ali Do you know nothing of our history?!

Sam None of the nationalities are on there!

Beth (*to Sam, aside*) Going well?

Sam Be nice.

Beth What school did you go to?

Sam Is it relevant?

Beth Maybe.

Sam Eton. I went to Eton.

Beth No! Did you actually?

Sam Don't say it like that. This isn't me coming out.

Beth What's that like?

Sam What do you mean?

Beth Eton, the Jungle. Bit of a leap.

Sam For the first time in my life no one cares where I come from.

Beth Were you in Slytherin?

Sam Very funny.

Beth Do I shake your hand?

Sam Shut up.

Beth Kiss your feet?

Sam You kiss my arse. (*Turning to the room.*) OK, everybody. Forget about quadrants! Kurdistan is Kurdistan. Sudan is Sudan. Afghanistan is Afghanistan. Above all we aim to be fair. We will distribute in proportion to population. I'm estimating that Sudan is the largest community.

Salar Afghanistan is the largest.

Mohammed We don't know that, Salar.

Sam Let's say they're equivalent?

Salar They're not.

Sam So, if I can build X number of houses a day, let's say, I'll start by building eighteen per cent in Afghanistan –

Salar Good.

Sam Eighteen per cent in Sudan.

Mohammed Yes.

Sam Fourty-four per cent in Eritrea, Iraq, Iran, Kurdistan, Syria. And the remaining twenty per cent divided correlatively between the minor nationalities.

Yasin Minor?

Sam By numbers. Any questions? Good. The second factor I've considered is need. Now, this falls under five sub-categories. Gender, age, illness or disability, time spent in the Jungle and the condition of your current dwelling. So, a woman with children will generally be housed before a single man. But a single man who has been here for five months, who has scabies, whose tent is flooded, may get a house before a single woman. Does that make sense?

Derek It's very good, Sam.

Sam I've weighted it. It's like an algorithm.

Helene Algorithm?

Sam Sorry, it's an English word –

Safi It's an Arabic word, actually.

The residents applaud this.

Sam It's an Arabic word, thank you, that means formula, an equation.

Ali What happens when the owner of house has good chance?

Sam When the owner of a house has good chance, it's reallocated to someone living in that person's quadrant. Sorry, country.

Safi How many houses can you build?

Sam Right now I'm on six a day. But if I can rely on your help, there's no reason I can't build a hunderd.

Derek Let's manage expectations here.

Helene How will they be built?

Sam I've streamlined production. We buy materials in bulk now, which saves money. We build the shelters in flat-pack off-site. Most of you are better builders than we are, so we bring the pieces in and you put them together yourselves.

Boxer enters holding a huge template of the flat-pack design.

Boxer has offered to lead on housing assembly.

Boxer Yeah, but I do have some conditions of employment. I don't like talking on the job. Especially in lilliput languages I don't understand. You want to natter, I'll see you in the bar after and I'm golden. But, at the end of the day, we're not here to make friends ot because we like each other. We're here because we have to be. Either because we've been forced or because we have a duty. Oh yeah, there's no grievance policy or any shite like that. If you don't like it, fuck off and get on with it. And don't touch my fucking toolbox.

Derek Thank you, Boxer.

Salar So the drunk man builds our houses.

Derek I think this system will work.

Sam This system will work.

Salar There are tensions here. Old wars.

Sam It's really quite complicated organising something like this. Fundraising, volunteers, vans, without . . . all of that.

Salar You ask us to forget?

Sam To be honest, it would be really helpful if you could.

Mohammed We are friends here.

Salar How old are you?

Sam Eighteen.

Salar One day I will tell you about my village in Afghanistan. You have destroyed it three times in the last two hundred years.

Mohammed Leave him alone, Salar.

Sam I've never destroyed your village.

Salar Your army has.

Sam My army?

Helene While you are talking, all Eritrean women are still in tents. A group of us have to sleep in the church because men tried to come in the night. Two of them are with child. The only protection we have is a whistle from Paula. We need strong wooden house with door and lock. We need now. Sam, when can we see your algorithm?

Sam You can't.

Salar Why not?

Sam It's in my head.

Helene So what are we supposed to do?

Car horns beep from the motorway.

Hamid Dugar! Dugar! Dugar!

Everyone looks to Hamid.

Dugar!

All residents of the camp rush out.

Boxer (*running out as well*) Du-bloody-gar! Come on, Derek. You've got to see this!

Derek Where are they going?

Safi Traffic jam on the motorway.

Pause.

Derek Well, in the circumstances I think that went rather well.

FIVE

THE TEST

Safi When does a place become a place? By November in the Jungle I could walk from Sudan through Palestine and Syria, pop into a Pakistani café on Oxford Street near Egypt, buy new shoes from the marketplace, Belgian cigarettes from an Iraqi cornershop, through Somalia, hot naan from the Kurdish baker, passing dentists, Eritrea, distribution points, Kuwait, hairdressers and legal centres, turn right on to François Hollande Street, turn left on to David Cameron's Avenue, stop at the sauna, catch a play in the theatre, service at the church, khutba in a mosque, before arriving at Salar's restaurant in Afghanistan. When does a place become home?

Night time. It's Salar's birthday. A cake is lit, and everyone sings.

Derek Salar, Salar, Salar. Do you remember that lovely man in the tweed jacket who ate here last week? You're not going to believe this but that was A.A. Gill, from the British newspaper the *Sunday Times*. But he wasn't reporting on the camp. He was writing a review of your restaurant. And this is what he had to say. Take it away, Mohammed.

Mohammed reads from a beautiful framed copy of the review.

Mohammed 'The room is a tent . . . with a make-do kitchen in one corner . . . But the dishes come hot and generous, with fluffy, nutty white rice . . . Then the surprise, the great surprise, is the chicken livers, they are perfect! This was a properly, cleverly crafted and wholly unexpected dish, made with a finesse that defied the surroundings, but at the same time elevated them . . .'

He gives it to Salar.

Happy Birthday, my friend.

Salar Four stars for atmosphere. Four stars for the food? I have five on Trip Advisor!

Norullah Thirteen stars!

Salar Alright, thank you. I don't know how you all found out –

Norullah I told them!

Salar Of course. Norullah, my restaurant man.

Cheers, as Salar blows the candles out. Shouts for a speech.

In Afghanistan many people do not know their birthday. Because of the wars, no one kept records. So, and this is true, I have – I had thirty-seven friends who all have their birthday on January 1st. But I am lucky. My mother wrote mine down. This is maybe the strangest place I have celebrated my birthday. And the strangest group of friends. But friends. Now get out my restaurant! There is a border to cross!

All Yayayayayayayaya!

People leave.

Paula Boxer?

Boxer Ey?

Paula You alright?

Boxer It's my little one's birthday today, an' all.

Paula Why didn't you go back?

Boxer Can't afford the ferry. Missus wouldn't have me anyway.

Paula You barmy bugger. You haven't called her, have you?

Boxer Lost my phone. Call this a fucking father?

Paula You're alright. Just lay off the Eritrean nightclub, yeah? Use this, call her now.

Boxer Cheers, Paula. You're a diamond.

Sam (*to Beth*) Do you want to stay in a hotel tonight?

Beth Sorry?

Sam A nice hotel. Nice-ish.

Beth Erm . . .

Sam Hear me out. We've been sleeping in tents for three months. My back's stiff –

Beth Is it?

Sam I've had the same stone in my spine for too long. I say nice-ish hotel. TV. Wifi. Remember that? Maybe a bottle of wine?

Beth I'm quite at home, thanks –

Sam Room service, the World Service? The option of having a bloody bath? There we are. You know you want a bath. I can see it in your eyes.

Beth No, you can't.

Sam We don't have to share a bed or anything, if that's –

Beth Say that again?

Sam I just mean, we can get a room with lots of beds. Three beds. Four beds, even! We can keep swapping in the night.

Beth Swapping?

Sam Forget it!

Beth Go on then.

Sam What?

Beth's phone rings.

Beth Hello? Sorry, who is this? Speak clearly.

Sam I'll go back to my tent.

Beth Who is this?

Sam And my stone.

Beth Shit. Where?

Sam My cold, hard stone.

Beth OK, stay calm. Don't say anything. Don't do anything. I'm coming.

Sam What is it?

Beth I need Safi.

Sam Why?

Pause.

Beth It's Okot. He's been arrested.

Outside the detention centre.

Safi (*French*) Excuse me, monsieur? I wonder if you can help me. I believe you are holding a young Sudanese boy who was detained two hours ago?

Guard (*French*) Name?

Safi Safi Al-Hussain.

Guard Passport?

Beth (*taking over*) I'm looking for a boy. He was arrested a few hours ago, in the tunnel.

Guard This is France, you speak French.

Beth OK . . . *Je suis . . . en train de . . . trouver quelqu'un.*

Guard British?

Beth *Oui. Je suis ici pour . . . voir un . . . jeune garçon.*

Guard *Non.*

Beth He's not in there.

Safi He's lying. Ask again.

Beth *Il est Sudanais . . . Il est détenu ici . . . Il est dix-sept ans.*

Guard *Nom?*

Beth Okot Sherif.

Guard *Comment?*

Beth Okot Sherif.

Guard *Non, comment vous appelez-vous?*

Beth Oh. Bethan James.

Guard Passport?

She gives him her passport. He leaves.

Beth *Est-il ici? Je dois le voir . . .* Fuck. I can't speak French.

The Guard returns with Okot, who is badly injured. Beth rushes to him.

Guard (*French*) Step back, back! (*English.*) Ten minutes.

The Guard leaves them.

Beth Okot, what the fuck? What happened?

He doesn't respond.

Have they asked how old you are?

Safi He said he's twenty.

Beth What? Why did you say that?

Safi If they think he's a child, they will force him to claim asylum in France.

Beth And if they think he's an adult they could deport him! Have you signed anything?

Safi They gave him a document.

Beth In French? Did you have a translator, a lawyer?

Safi That must be a joke, Beth.

Beth Did you sign it? Okot?

Okot Yes.

Beth Why would you do that?

The Guard re-enters.

Guard You must go now.

Beth We're not finished. You said ten minutes.

Guard There is problem. You must leave.

Beth This is madness!

Guard (*French*) Now!

Beth I'm not leaving!

Guard I've told you, you are in France, you speak French.

Beth This is not France! He's a seventeen-year-old boy! Look at him! This is not France! You've forced him to sign documents! He doesn't speak French! He should have a translator, that's the law. This is not France. I have friends. Lawyers. Human rights lawyers. In Paris. And if I call them they are going to come down on you so hard. No translator, forced to sign, seventen years old, cuts, bruises all over his body. Where did he get those? There's a European Convention on the Rights of the Child, don't you dare say this is France! I'm serious. Look at me. I will make your life hell. We're walking out of here today, now. I don't care what he's signed. You're going to rip it up and let him go.

The Guard looks her up and down.

Guard OK.

Beth Excuse me?

Guard Go! And if I see him again, you won't.

He throws Beth's passport to the floor.

(*French.*) Now get the fuck out.

They step out of the detention centre.

Beth Fuck. I don't know anyone in Paris.

Pause.
Okot picks up Beth's passport.

Okot. Do you want to stay in a hotel tonight?

Safi Beth, you know it's illegal in France to stay in a hotel without papers.

Beth I know.

Safi And it's against the law to aid refugees.

Beth Yeah, thanks, Safi.

Safi You should take some time to think about this.

Okot hands Beth her passport.

Let's have an interval.

Interval.

A hotel room.

Safi The Hotel Meurice, Calais. (*To Beth.*) You know it's illegal to stay in a hotel without papers.

Beth I know.

Safi And it's against the law in France to aid refugees.

Beth Yeah, thanks, Safi.

Safi OK.

Beth (*to Okot*) Stay here.

She goes into the bathroom to get a bowl of water. Okot is left alone with Safi.

Safi Do you want to talk? Talking sometimes helps.

Okot If I talk to her. You think she would understand?

Safi I think she could. Talk to her. Tell her.

Okot takes his top off. His whole body is badly scarred. Beth re-enters.

Beth Oh my God.

Okot I am dead.

Beth What?

Okot Dead.

Beth You're not dead. You're here with me.

Okot A refugee dies many times.

Beth I know.

Okot You know?

Beth I didn't mean that. I mean I can imagine.

A long pause.

Okot What do you know of me?

Beth You're from Sudan.

Okot Where?

Beth Darfur?

Okot What do you know of Darfur?

Beth There are lots of problems in Darfur.

Okot What problems?

Beth A genocide . . . When . . . an entire people is . . .

Okot A people?

Beth A race or religion. When a people is –

Okot People is your father. People is your mother. What do you know about Mediterranean?

Beth I know about the boats.

He is silent. She is forced to continue. She is uneasy.

The boats are tiny. Too many people are put inside. By the smugglers. Lots of the boats sink. It's obviously really dangerous. Thousands of people try to cross every day. It's tragic.

Silence.

It's a tragedy.

Silence.

I don't know.

Okot Sahara is more dangerous. You are in a truck six days and six nights. If truck breaks down, you die. If you fall out, you die. If you run out of water, you die. If militia find you, you die. If you don't keep warm at night, you die. If I die in the Sahara my body is never found. Six days, six nights.

Beth You survived?

Okot I survive with my uncle.

Safi He thought he was his uncle.

Okot I have never been this far from my mother . . . I cannot be boy any more . . . That was my first death.

Beth If this is too difficult, Okot –

Okot You know about Libya?

Beth No.

Okot You must know about Libya! Everyone about Libya say same thing: Libya is worst place in world! Everyone has gun. Big problems for black people. But at least we are here. One step further.

Beth That's good.

Safi Go on.

Okot In Tripoli you look for middleman.

Safi You know this word? Middleman.

Okot He takes you to the smuggler. The smuggler pays him. And you pay smuggler. Some people pay $2,000. We pay $400. I thought this was fair! Pay what you can! I thought we go to harbour. But no. They send us to *mazraa*.

Safi Compound. Warehouse.

Okot It is prison. Out of city. Nowhere away. You know it as maybe . . . (*To Safi, in Arabic.*) Hell?

Safi Hell.

Okot *Mazraa*. They keep you. Two months, maybe.
Little food, little water. Shit-place in corner. Torture.
I have seen men do to the teeth. Slice this muscle on
thumb. Flip coin to choose which toe. And other things
you canot know.
   I lose my uncle here also . . . I get to know my uncle.

Safi It's not his uncle.

Okot For women, it is even more difficult. You know.
I know you know, because now you are scared. You are
scared to think *mazraa*.

Safi She doesn't know. They don't know.

Okot Your mind cannot think.

Safi Do you think we'd be here if they knew?

Okot They lie me down. Lift concrete stone on my back,
heavy. They make video on my phone to send to my
mother to see. I must ask her for more money. More
money, more, more, more! I think of my mother . . .
I think of Darfur . . .
   Darfur is the most beautiful place in world. Have you
seen the sun rise in Darfur?

Beth No . . .

   Pause.

Okot You never need to see it rise again. My mother is
like librarian. She takes books around town and villages,
and we sing and eat aseeda and shorbet adas . . .
(*Arabic.*) Everyone in all the villages knows her. The
children run out to see her, sit with her.

Beth What is he saying?

Safi He's speaking about his mother.

Okot (*Arabic*) She teaches them reading and writing.

Safi She teaches reading and writing.

Okot (*Arabic*) She was mother to everyone. She lit up the room. She was an angel.

Safi She was a mother to everyone. She lit up the room. She was an angel.

Pause.

Okot Last time I saw my mother she was crying. You have seen your mother cry?

Beth Yes.

Okot Me too. But never like this.

Safi Tell her about Magareefna.

Okot I am with my mother to Magareefna.

Safi A nearby village.

Okot We are riding on bus together, twenty minutes.

Safi February 8th. This year.

Okot Men on horses block road. Surround us. They bang on windows, shake bus from side to side . . . Janjaweed come in and shoot the driver.

Safi Government militia.

Okot They take us out on to roadside. Women are separated from men, and the women . . .

Safi Tell her.

Okot With guns they make us watch.

Safi After, they burn Magareefna to ashes, and over the next two days eighteen more villages.

Okot This is genocide.

Safi The *Janjaweed* use women to target men. If Okot leaves, his mother is safer.

Okot I don't want to go.

Safi You had to. For her.

Okot A man arrives who I have never seen before. My mother say he is my uncle. She give him $400. All the money she has. She has nothing more.
I think of her watching the video. I am pressed against ground, the stone cuts into my back.
She will be crying. She has nothing more, she cannot pay. I think of her watching the video.
Second death.

Pause.

Safi Finally you are taken to the boats, yes?

Okot Yes.

Safi The coastguard has been paid. The local militia. Was it a big boat?

Okot Small boat.

Safi Rubber?

Okot Yes.

Safi A zodiac. Fifty people. You are given a package with a balloon to put your phone in, GPS device, a life jacket.

Salar If you are lucky.

Safi You hope the life jacket is real.

Salar You pray the life jacket is real.

Ali Real or not, fifteen dinar for package.

Okot I am in first boat.

79

Safi The first?

Norullah Big problem.

Okot We go out to bigger boat.

Ali A fishing trawler. Fifteen metres long. Wooden. Strong.

Yasin But old.

Safi Painted black so the coastguard can't see.

Okot The less money you pay, the worse your place on the boat. Pay what you can. Now you know.

Beth Yes. Now I know.

Safi Rich people go on top deck.

Mohammed Poor people go underneath. Below sea level. In the hold.

Okot I am pushed down near engine. It is going in my face.

Safi The zodiacs keep coming. This boat is for two hundred people.

Maz Here there are seven hundred.

Hamid Nine hundred.

Omid Fifteen hundred.

Okot People on top of people on top of people.

Felah The heat is unbearable.

Safi No smugglers make this journey, do you know this? You are left alone.

Ali Point in direction and go.

Okot Stay still or boat will sink.

Ali Wait for international waters, then phone for help.

Okot Suddenly I am thinking I shouldn't be here. I try to get out. I shout. I cannot move. I hear water outside. I cannot swim.

Omid I cannot swim.

Hamid I cannot swim.

Okot If boat has problem I am dead.

Helene comes forward with Little Amal, singing gently.

Mohammed All of below, we are dead.

Okot Pressed to me is mother and daughter. She is maybe three years old. I think what will she remember? Mother is singing to stop tears.

People join in with their own prayers.

Why is everyone singing?

Safi They are not singing. They are praying.

Okot Suddenly I am praying.

He recites a prayer.

Safi If you stand on the shores at night of Lesvos or Kos, you hear this sound from the boats, like the sea itself is praying.

Okot A man cries out loud. And at moment of his most tears, he shits. He has tight teeth and is shamed for what has happened. He tries to say sorry but he cannot stop crying. A girl is sick. So another person is sick. So I am sick.

Beth Okot!

Okot Panic causes the boat to tip. The tip causes more panic. Shouts of leak. Maybe it is piss. Please be piss.

Salar It is not piss.

Okot Then the floor turns around and hundreds of bodies spin in the hold.

Mohammed Water rushes in.

Norullah A man shouts. 'Take off your shoes!'

Norullah *and* **Maz** 'Take off your shoes!'

Okot I rip my trousers off because a man is holding on to me. Another man is pushing up against the door.

Yasin Push! Push!

Okot The door swings out.

Safi Five minutes he is under the water.

Okot Five minutes.

Safi Think.

Okot I am dead. Third death.

   Safi recites a prayer.

Real death.

Safi You want to ask a question?

Beth How did you survive?

Helene We didn't.

Beth But you're here now.

Okot This is not us.

Safi We're different now. New.

Okot Why are you here, Beth?

Mohammed Why are you not at your home?

Safi What can we give you?

Okot Before, I could give you anything. I could give you myself.

Helene What do we have now?

Okot This journey. This story.

Safi And you have heard this story before. A thousand times, I am sure.

Okot Now you know. It isn't me, but now it is me.

Safi's phone rings. He gives it to Beth, who answers.

Beth Hello . . . Shit, what . . .? I can't . . . What? I'm coming.

She exits as many phones ring.

Safi Friday 13th of November, in the Jungle, a Sudanese man in his wooden house wrapped himself in blankets and fell asleep with a lit candle. It accidentally set fire to half the camp.

On the same night, in Paris, terrorists walked into restaurants, a stadium, a theatre and murdered 130 people. The deadliest attack in France since the Second World War.

It was reported that the two events were connected. They were not. It was also reported that a Syrian refugee passport was found with the body of one of the attackers. It was fake. But does it matter?

In that moment, the refugee, terror, the Jungle and me, were bound together. Alan Kurdi changed everything, and the night of the 13th of November changed everything again.

The horror I escaped had found me.

A vigil.
    Signs reading #Pray4Paris are lifted.
    A minute of silence ends.

Safi Thank you, everyone. I am writing an open letter, from all the citizens of the Jungle, condemning the attacks –

Boxer It's got nothing to do with you lot.

Safi We know this –

Boxer You're running from the same people what did it!

Safi And this is what the letter will say.

Boxer Oh, for fuck's sake –

Derek Thank you, Boxer. Mohammed?

Mohammed Thank you, Derek. The pictures I see in the news, I recognise. It is Darfur. I know the pain. It is why I'm here.

Salar It is the streets of Kabul.

Hamid Basra.

Ali Halabja.

Yasin Gaza City.

Safi Aleppo.

Mohammed Today we are all Paris. Now more than ever we must stand together. The fire means many Sudanese people are homeless. I want to thank Salar for opening his restaurant in our time of need.

Norullah I have tent for black boy.

Mohammed Okot. His name is Okot. Thank you, Norullah. Without this humanity, we would be lost.

Norullah There is space next to mine.

Maz (*Pashto*) What are you doing, brother?

Norullah gives Okot the tent.

84

Safi Thank you, Mohammed.

Derek Thank you, Norullah.

Safi Does anyone else have any reflections?

Paula Last night was an absolute clusterfuck.

Derek Paula.

Paula Children nearly died. What happened to our plans? Why were people firefighting? Make breaks! That's it. We could have saved more homes. It's a miracle we didn't lose someone.

Derek There are lessons to learn, of course –

Paula No candles in a shanty town made of wood –

Safi Let's stay calm.

Paula This can never happen again.

Ali What about the rumours?

Helene What rumours?

Ali That the fire was not an accident. My boys saw a group of men running down Rue de Garrennes.

Helene Safi, take control of this.

Salar Local fascists meet on this road every night. They attack with metal bars.

Boxer Fuckers.

Ali We take group of men and meet them tonight.

Derek *and* **Safi** No, no, no!

Derek Do not do that. We do not know what caused this fire.

Paula Whatever caused it, things need to change. Volunteers were drunk, fucked-up on fuck knows what. I'm not naming names –

Boxer Oh, fuck off, Paula!

Derek There is a time and a place.

Salar He was asleep in my restaurant while the fire was burning. Children were screaming and he was on the floor.

Safi Salar, please –

Paula Salar, I'll deal with him. (*To Boxer, shouting.*) Get a grip or fuck off! (*To everyone.*) Has anyone been to a proper UN refugee camp? They have staff. Rotas. Plans in place for shit like last night.

Derek This is not a UN refugee camp –

Paula Too fucking right it's not!

Derek This is us! And some credit is due for how we managed.

Helene Safi, do something!

Safi What do you think I'm trying to do, Helene?

Helene This is not good enough.

Safi Listen, everyone –

Salar France is in a state of emergency. The police have more power. They closed the borders. Last night was nearly Jungle finished.

Safi Salar, we have to –

Salar Let me speak. Refugees: remember why you are here. Good chance may soon be no chance. And volunteers. –

Mohammed Do not divide us, Salar!

Salar We have trusted you with our lives. If you are here for opportunity, or holiday, or because this place is better than your home, leave. We do not want you. The last thing Zhangal needs is more refugees.

A thunderclap, and it starts to rain. Hard.

Paula And that's all we need.

People begin to disperse.

Derek Rest everyone. Stay dry. Stay strong. Don't lose hope. Safi, you need to get that letter out as soon as possible.

Safi I'm collecting the signatures.

Sam Safi, I need a meeting to plan the rebuild of Sudan tomorrow.

Safi Slow down, Sam.

Sam Real roads, shelters, irrigation, proper town planning –

Safi You need to be careful here.

Sam We don't have time to be careful. I'm starting tomorrow with every volunteer.

Salar Enjoy your new houses, Mohammed.

Maz (*Pashto*) Keep away from the black boy.

Safi Maz.

Salar Don't get involved.

Maz Keep away from fucking black boy.

Salar Maz, kitchen. Norullah, you do not go to school any more.

Safi is left alone, shaken.

The Women and Children's Centre.
Paula, Helene and Little Amal are sorting boxes of donations.

Beth I need to get a boy out.

Paula Beth.

Beth He's falling apart.

Paula Beth, we haven't got a single kid over yet under Dublin III.

Beth Why not? You've been talking about it for months.

Paula Why do you think? Mother-fucking Theresa is fighting it in the courts.

Beth But it's the law!

Boxer (*entering, carrying a box of donations*) Where do you want this?

Paula One more step and I'll chop your bollocks off.

Boxer You what?

Paula Women and Children's Centre. Clue's in the name.

Boxer I'm bloody helping.

Paula You're atoning. Now piss off and empty the toilets.

She chucks him a bottle of bleach and some filthy marigolds.

Boxer (*exiting*) Charming.

Paula I think everyone needs to calm the fuck down.

She lights a cigarette.

Deep breath . . . Now doesn't that feel better? Helene, why don't you tell Beth your news?

Helene I claim asylum in France.

Beth What?

Paula Finally, something to celebrate.

Helene I hoped for smuggle, but since what happened in Paris price is too high. And I won't pay the other way.

Beth What do you mean?

Paula What do you think?

Beth So you're leaving the Jungle?

Helene No. In France you do not get house for a long time.

Beth You've claimed asylum but you still have to live here?

Paula Fucking ridiculous. But at least it means you won't be trying any more. No more trains or lorries. No more smugglers.

Beth How do the smugglers work, Helene?

Helene You pay them and they take you to UK.

Beth Yeah, but how?

Helene You find the right one for you.

Beth There are different ones?

Helene Different smugglers for each nationality. Afghans for Afghans, Africans for Africans, Albanians will take anyone but they are no good. Kurdish smugglers are the best. Like business class. Five-star journey to UK.

Beth Why?

Helene They control the best areas. They have arrangements with best drivers who drive best lorries.

Beth Do you pay cash?

Helene Yes . . .

Beth You carry all that money?

Helene You volunteers are so funny. You think we sew into the seams of our clothes? I have bank account!

Beth How do you find them?

Paula Why are you so interested?

Beth We have no idea what's actually happening here. This whole fucking crisis.

Paula Oh, come on, Beth. It's only a crisis because we're calling it that. A million people, Europe shits her knickers. Population of seven hundred million, that's nought point fuck knows per cent. Go to Jordan, quarter of people are refugees. Lebanon, it's a third. Crisis? European governments need to stop breaking their own laws, and then we need to stop our obsession with helping.

Helene You think we don't need help?

Paula Look at this place! Give people a chance, a hammer, some nails, build a city in a day! You're better than we are. Smarter. Braver. We're the ones who need fucking help.

Helene So why are you here?

Paula For the children.

Helene And the adults?

Paula Come on, you know what I think about this. If we can't even win the argument about unaccompanied kids like her, we don't stand a chance with you.

Little Amal groans.

Helene Paula thinks I am economic migrant.

Paula No, that's not what I think.

Helene Paula thinks I made a choice. Sure, my life was not about to end in Eritrea, but why should I spend it all in military service building roads, like my sister? She is the smartest woman, but she will never be free. I did not want this to happen for me so am I not still refugee?

Paula Helene, anyone who traipses across a desert, across an ocean on a fucking lilo will always have my support, you know that. But the kids are different. She doesn't have the capacity to choose any of this.

Helene I didn't choose my life, Paula.

Paula Not the choice to flee Eritrea. The choice to come this far.

Beth I don't understand.

Paula 'Claim asylum in the first safe country you come to.'

Helene I didn't claim asylum in Italy, where I landed, because they treat refugee like animal. My cousin is in UK. I speak English. Everyone in Eritrea does, because UK used to run Eritrea! And for refugee, UK laws are best in Europe.

Beth Why have the best laws if the only way to access them is to jump on a moving train?

Helene I thought the Jungle was France. But it's not. The fences, the barbed wire, the police beating children, it is all paid for by UK.

Beth Hang on, what? Is that true?

Paula Sixty million quid so far.

Helene UK was my dream since I was child. But now I hear from my cousin things are changing. Someone spat at her in the street outside her church in Kings Cross. For the first time since Eritrea she is frightened. I cannot live in a place that treats a person like this. It is why I have to claim asylum in France.

Paula You made the right choice, Helene.

Helene There is no choice. And that is why I do not feel like celebrating today.

Beth There's this journalist. James Bartholomew. He made up a phrase in a magazine article. About refugees, actually. Virtue-signalling. When people share opinions or petitions or crowdfunders online, he says all you're really doing is signalling your virtue. You're not actually doing anything. And within a week it had been picked up by every newspaper in the world. It'll be in the dictionary this time next year, I guarantee it.

Paula Wanker.

Beth Exactly. First I thought, what a wanker. Cynical world. What sorry state have we got ourselves into if we can't honestly express our horror at what is happening? That you can't cry at the picture of a boy, dead on a beach, without some fucker telling you you're lying. But, you know, I remember going on a school trip to Parliament. I remember watching a debate. I remember being so fucking awestruck by this incredible place with all the laws we've ever made. I believed in it, too, Helene, like you. But now I know, and I am so, so sorry. That's the virtue signal. Look at us. Look how much we care. These people have human rights! They do exist! Until they're standing at our door, screaming for help. The British government. The French government. The United Nations. The European fucking Union. Where the fuck are you?

Pause.

If the system won't save him, fuck the system. Do it yourself.

She leaves.

Paula Beth! Fuck's sake.

Helene goes to leave.

Where are you going?

Helene Church. Carol service.

Paula Oh, fuck. It's fucking Christmas.

Boxer enters with his banjo.

Not now, banjo.

Boxer Nah, nah, I'm atoning.

Paula Jesus, what have I started?

Boxer I've cleaned the bogs, and now I'm handing out Christmas shoe boxes kindly donated by the Great British Public.

Paula I hope you've washed your hands.

Boxer (*singing to the tune of 'The Blaydon Races'*)

It's Christmas in the Jungle, so it's time for something
    pleasant.
Court'sy of the British public, everbody's gettin'
    a present,
So gather your Christmas jumpers, your handbags
    and your socks,
Cos ev'ry school in ev'ry county in the country's sent
    a shoe box.

Theresa May, look inside your wardrobe,
I'm sure you could donate a pair of leopard-print
    stilettos.

That lovely piece of leatherwear from 1980 fuck knows,
You'll miss it for a little while but think how far the
    thought goes.

What do you reckon?

Paula I've heard better.

Boxer Well, work in progress. (*Handing a shoebox to*
Little Amal.) Here you go, pet, how's about this.

Continues singing:

The look upon her face when she sees the Nikey box.
Score! I've got myself some Airs, a brand new pair
    of high tops.
She rips it up and looks inside, it's 'Haddaway again!'
A packet of pantie liners and some Nivea for Men!

(*Giving Little Amal a Snickers bar.*) Here you go, love.
A Snickers bar. That's more like it.

Pause.

I hope you haven't got a peanut allergy. And this one's
for you, Paula.

Theresa May, look across the water.
We've got loads of children here, they're all for the
    slaughter.
You call yourself a Christian, you're more a prison
    warder.
Just imagine how you'd feel . . . if this one was your
    daughter.

Paula Atoned.

She high-fives him.

Now piss off, Geordie Dylan. (*To Little Amal.*) Come
on, darling.

*They all leave together. For a moment they look like a
family.*
   Maz walks in playing the harmonica.
   Sam takes Henri on a tour of the Jungle.
   *Throughout the following dialogue, songs from
many cultures can be heard throughout the Jungle.
   A hymn from the church.*

Sam This is Afghanistan. I've built six hundred houses
here. The Afghan High Street is the civic centre of the
camp, where most of the restaurants and cafes are. Over
here, Sudan. We're rebuilding after the fire. Then I want
to build a new area by the motorway. The people of
Calais should see this.

Henri The people of Calais have been seeing this for
twenty-five years. Imagine what that does to a place.
Where is that music coming from?

Sam One of the churches.

Henri You're building a city.

Sam It's becoming ordered.

Henri It's becoming permanent. You're building it to last.

Sam Because the problem is not going to disappear.

Henri They're not here because of my border, Sam.
They're here because of yours. If we ripped up the Treaty
of Le Touquet today, this Jungle would move to Dover
tomorrow.

Sam This would never happen in Britain.

Henri Are you so sure about that?

Sam We all have responsibility for this.

Henri For what, Sam? Responsibility for what?

   *An Arabic song from a mosque, celebrating Mawlid,
   the birth of the Prophet Mohammed.*

You're giving these people not only everything they need, but anything they want. You're making it appealing.

Sam Anyone who comes here and calls this place appealing has a problem.

Henri What are they singing now?

Sam They're celebrating the Prophet Mohammed's birthday. It falls on Christmas Eve this year.

Henri You think I'm cruel because I don't help these people in the way that you want. But I don't want to go to bed at night thinking my actions have persuaded someone from, let's say, from Afghanistan to get inside a rubber boat expecting to find happiness here. You give them false hope, Sam. So you tell me who is cruel?

Norullah enters, chased by Maz.

Maz I fucking told you not to help black boy!

Norullah I only come for fucking food.

Maz For black Sudan! He already gets everything!

Okot Norullah.

Norullah (*to Okot*) He's fucking crazy, man.

Maz Hey, fuck you! I'm not fucking crazy!

Maz pulls a knife out.

You want to see crazy? I show you fucking crazy, black boy.

He chases Norullah out of the restaurant.

Maz (*Pashto*) You bring shame to Afghanistan. I see you again I'll fucking slit you.

Salar (*entering, Pashto*) Maz. What are you doing? Give me the knife. This is your boy. I know you're upset. I feel it too. But this is not the way to UK. Go.

Maz exits.

How long before you start building in Afghanistan, Sam?

Sam When I've finished in Sudan.

Salar My boys are angry. They are saying you favour black man.

Sam Tell them I treat everyone fairly.

Salar I say this every day. I promise you, soon there will be riots. (*To Henri.*) Who the fuck are you? Nice shoes.

Salar exits.

Sam Salar. Community leader of Afghanistan.

Henri This isn't a city. It's a bomb.

Sam Nobody wants violence here. That's our common ground. So let's work together. Meet and talk regularly. I know there are tensions between the communities, but I can keep them under control if I know what you're planning.

Henri How long do you think you have here?

Sam I was hoping you would tell me. At least until March.

Henri Why do you say that?

Sam You can't make people homeless in winter. That's French law.

The Call to Prayer is heard.

Henri This, this isn't France.

Sam Six months? A year?

Henri You're very impressive for an eighteen-year-old.

Sam What do you think?

Little Amal hands Henri a scarf.

Henri I would need to be discreet.

Sam (*holding out his hand*) So would I. It will be a good thing.

Derek enters with Safi. They are both tipsy, holding cans of beer.

Henri (*shaking Sam's hand, then leaving*) Don't build by the motorway. That's all I can say. Happy Christmas.

'Jerusalem' is heard in the distance.

Derek Not gone home?

Sam Thought I'd rather stay here.

Derek Friend of yours? Wait. Listen. Jerusalem was a place like this once. All the great cities. They all started the same way. It's just a group of people, waiting by a river, the sea.

Sam Derek –

Derek You are doing something amazing, Sam.

More songs can be heard from around the camp. They grow together, discordantly.

Of course there are problems, there always are at the beginning. But give us five years. That's all we need. We can build it here.

Sam Build what?

Derek The dream, Sam. What are we waiting for? Eh? You, me, Safi. I mean, look at him. Look at Safi. No one wants you over there. No offence. But it's the truth. You are not welcome.

Sam Derek, you're being rude.

Derek No, he needs to know, Sam. You need to know that this is as good as it's ever going to get for you.

Sam I think it's time for bed.

Sam tries to lead Derek away.

Derek No, no, no. Don't touch me. Boy. Who was that man? You need to be careful. Those people, they hate us. There will come a time when all this is threatened. When they come – and they will come – you need to know whose side you're on. You need to know what you're defending. When they come . . . When sorrows come . . .

Safi When sorrows come, they come not single spies, but in battalions.

Sam takes Derek off.
   The music stops.
   Salar rips Safi's can away.

Salar You've had enough. You're no good to anyone like this. We need you, Safi. What the fuck is wrong with you?

He exits.

Safi It's one thing ending a year in the Jungle. It's another starting a new one.

Norullah enters with a huge dead bird, a snow crane. It's beautiful. Long, thin, orange legs. Its neck dangles down, almost touching the mud.

Safi What's that?

Norullah Bird.

Safi What bird?

Norullah (*Pashto*) Snow crane. (*English.*) We have in Afghanistan.

Safi You found it?

Norullah I killed it.

Safi Crazy Afghan.

Norullah Wanna see something crazy?

He takes a gun out. Points it at Safi.

Merry Christmas.

Safi Fuck, Norullah.

Norullah You scared now?

Safi Where did you get that from?

Norullah Bought it. Kurdistan.

He mimes shooting the gun.

Maz tries cut me. BANG! Salar make me go shop.
BANG! France police destroy my house. BANG!

Points the gun back at Safi.

You scared now.

Safi Yes, I'm scared.

Norullah We're all going to die here! We're not going
to get to UK! Fuck police. Fuck Jungle. Bang! Fucking
fence, bang! Fucking France, bang! Fucking Afghanistan,
bang! Fucking Mujahideen, bang! Fucking Taliban,
bang! Fucking rain, bang! Fucking cold, bang! Fucking
sick! Sick of being bambino! Fuck you, UK!

*He shoots the gun towards the cliffs of Dover, then
holds the gun to his own head.*

Fucking bambino in fucking Jungle.

Okot enters.

Okot Yes. Bambino who crossed desert, seven days.
Bambino who swam to shore when boat was drowning.

Norullah (*Pashto*) Shut up.

Okot Bambino who was beaten in prison, three nights, in Hungary.

Norullah Shut up!

Okot Bambino who crossed eleven borders. Bambino who –

Norullah Fucking shut up, black man!

He points the gun at Okot.

Okot Bambino who walked here. Alone. Five thousand miles. You. Norullah.

Norullah lowers the gun.

Norullah Why my mother say go UK? Why UK no want me?

Okot I do not want UK. I want home. I want Sudan. But we cannot go back. No chance. There is only the trying. 'Why my mother say go UK?' Look at those cliffs, Norullah, look. They are so close. We just have to get there. Then Jungle, all of this, will be old life. And then I know we cannot die again. Let's go to the motorway. Let's go try.

Norullah Try . . .

Safi Try.

They run off towards the motorway.

Safi It's one thing starting a new year in the Jungle. It's another not knowing if it will ever end.

Omar (*entering*) My friend. So cold.

Safi I know.

Omar My friend. Coat?

Safi What?

Omar Your coat.

Safi I don't have anything else.

Omar I think . . . I die here tonight.

Safi stares blankly at him. Then takes off his coat and gives it to Omar. He stands freezing in nothing but a T-shirt.

Beth Safi.

Ali's caravan.

Ali Why are you here, Beth?

Beth He's called Okot.

Ali In the Jungle.

Beth I don't really have time –

Ali I like to know the people I'm going to work with.

Safi Beth runs the school.

Ali Oh, I've heard about the school. You are a charity person then. We are very similar.

Beth You're a smuggler.

Safi Beth, you can't –

Ali No, Safi, it's fine. (*To Omid, in Farsi.*) Turn the lights on. (*To Beth.*) You British always use this word. Like we are in the business of moving tobacco. It was the same fifteen years ago, at Sangatte. I remember all the British volunteers then. The same angry faces. I should say thank you for making this place comfortable for my clients while they wait. A school. Wonderful. Thank you, Beth.

Beth If you're not a smuggler, what are you?

Ali I am freedom fighter. Peshmerga. Army of Kurdistan. You know what this word means? Those who face death. Everyone here has lost their home. I am here because the Kurdish people never had one. This is our fight, and we find no help from your governments. They are happy to see refugee die as long as he is wearing new shoes. I help refugee find a home. I fight for real freedom. You would do the same.

Beth And take their money.

Ali Yes, I make money. But most of it goes back to Erbil in the fight against Daesh. Yes.

Pause.

You are very suspicious of me.

Beth I think this whole situation is because of you.

Ali Because of smugglers? Once I was the only way a man could ever dream of arriving on your shore. Now he opens the map on his phone, zooms out, and thinks, 'It's not too far, it's close enough to walk.' And he sets off on the journey of his life. It is not about this border. It's the border in here. (*Tapping his head.*) That is gone now. Come. Sit. Tell me about Okot.

Beth What do you want to know?

Ali Black boy?

Beth Sudanese.

Ali Child?

Beth Seventeen.

Ali Why him?

Beth Do I need a reason?

Ali There are many boys in the Jungle.

Beth He doesn't have anyone else. Are you going to help or not?

Ali This doesn't happen. A British volunteer coming to me. But for a friend of Safi's . . . A thousand.

Beth Shit.

Safi It's a good price.

Beth Thank you.

Ali Thank me when I have helped him.

He hands his phone to her. She types her number in.

I'll call you. One week, maybe. Friday, maybe.

Beth What will happen?

Ali We give him an onion. We put him in a box. And I'll shut the door myself, how does that sound?

Beth An onion?

Ali For the guard dogs. The smell keeps them away. I like you, Beth. You are trying to understand. But you can't. I will give your friend his freedom.

Beth Let's go.

Safi I think I'll stay.

Beth (*leaving*) Ok . . .

Ali Impressive girl.

Safi Is that true about the onion?

Ali Safi, I'm expensive for a reason.

Safi You will help her, won't you?

Ali Where is your coat?

Safi I left it.

Ali You gave it away.

Safi I didn't.

Ali You'll freeze to death. When are you going to stop this? This act. The man who helps.

A gunshot in the distance.

Someone's having fun.

Safi No, Ali, things are changing, and you don't you see it. The children are losing their minds. One of them has a gun. For all I know you sold it to him.

Ali You look tired.

Safi Angry, Ali. I feel angry. I thought this was a place, but it's not. It's between places. It doesn't exist. We're in burzakh, purgatory, waiting on the Judgement, in perfect view of the motorway, for everyone to see. A warning to the world. Don't come. Don't try. Refugees, migrants, whatever we fucking are. But not people, Ali. We're between people. Drowning in this sea of suffering, and you're blind to it because you're swimming in it, you're fucking fishing in it. Freedom fighter? If you were a freedom fighter, you'd be there fighting for that freedom. But you're not, because you're scared, like me, like everyone here. Scared to fight, scared to die.

Pause.

I'm terrified, Ali. I admitted that to a child today. But at least I can admit it . . .

Ali We can't all be good men like you.

Safi recites a line of ancient Arabic poetry, which Ali translates.

'The worst of life's tricks is the enemy who must be your best friend.' Don't quote poetry at me, Safi. Sit. I am not your enemy.

Safi You're not my friend either.

Ali Don't you think it might be time? You, my friend, are the only person who would find this decision difficult.

Safi I have to leave, Ali. I will kill myself by staying.

Pause.

Ali No guilt.

Safi No.

Ali You have been a good man.

Safi Fuck, no.

Ali And now it is your time. I'll call you. Be ready.

Ali exits with Omid and Hamid.

Safi I can't begin another yeah here, Ali. You understand that, don't you?

SEVEN
THE GREAT MOVE

Chaos in Salar's restaurant.

Derek Right. Can I have everyone's attention, please. We are going to explain as clearly as we can the facts as we know them. This morning, a notice was posted by the police –

Salar Jungle finished?

Sam No, the Jungle is not finished.

Salar But we are being evicted?

Sam We have to stay calm, Salar.

Derek Do we have translators?

Salar Forget about translators! Tell us what it says!

Paula Can someone fucking read it?

Sam I'm trying. It's from the court in Lille. 'The regular incursions of migrants on to the road is posing a threat to public safety.'

Boxer Du-fucking-gar.

Sam It gives police the authority to clear a one hundred metre strip of land around the entire perimeter of the Jungle.

Uproar.

Paula How is this legal? It's winter.

Sam It's legal under State of Emergency laws.

Paula Oh, for fuck's sake.

Mohammed What does 'clear' mean?

Derek It means the police will come with bulldozers –

Sam Derek!

Derek And destroy everything in the eviction zone.

Sam You can't call it that!

Mohammed So it is an eviction.

Sam No, it's a relocation.

Derek Sam, we have to be honest here.

Sam This can be a relocation, if we want it to be.

Mohammed What is in the eviction zone?

Sam The term they are using is 'buffer zone'.

Sam draws a line down the middle of the restaurant.

This means a line that extends all the way to Chemin des Dunes in that direction, and to the north in that direction. Everything on this side of the line is safe. Everything on this side of the line will be cleared by police.

Cries fill the restaurant.

We only have one option. We move everything from that side of the line to that side of line, before the police arrive.

Salar When will they arrive?

Sam Friday morning.

Derek At dawn.

Boxer Three days?!

Mohammed That's thousands of people.

Sam We think around two thousand people. Eight hundred houses.

Paula Sam, it's not possible.

Boxer We designed them to be moved.

Paula Eight hundred? In three days?

Sam We have to make it possible.

Boxer If it has to be done it has to be done. We'll just have to work harder.

Sam Thank you, Boxer. We have to. It's our only choice.

Salar It is not our only choice. We can resist.

Sam We can't, Salar. Resistance is impossible.

Salar You have drawn the line down the middle of my restaurant.

Pause.

Derek So we have a choice to make.

Sam No, we don't!

Derek We can collaborate with the authorities –

Sam Co-operate, Derek. We can co-operate!

Derek Move everything from the eviction zone. Do their work for them. Set a precedent for any future eviction they want to throw at us –

Sam Derek!

Derek Or we can say no. Sit tight. Protest the notice. You have to decide. We will support the choice you make.

Mohammed We need time to consult our communities.

Derek Let's meet here again in one hour.

People leave.

Sam (*to Derek*) Derek, we have to stop this.

Derek You can't force them.

Sam We know what the CRS will do!

Derek They have every right to resist the destruction of their home.

Sam Their houses won't be destroyed if we move them!

Derek Their home, Sam! Not houses! This is bigger than houses, bigger than the Jungle. I'm sorry to say it, but you don't understand that, and you don't know what it means to resist.

Sam Because I'm young.

Derek Because nothing you hold dear has ever been threatened.

Sam Fuck you, Derek! This is not a good place! It isn't something to be preserved!

Derek The Diggers, the Chartists, the Suffragettes, the Miners, Greenham Common.

Sam Oh, come on!

Derek You stand on the shoulders of giants, and you don't even know who they are! These people are the strangers of the world. Bombed, abused, humiliated.

Sam I hadn't noticed.

Derek (*leaving*) This might be their time.

Sam (*following Derek*) Derek, Derek . . .

Henri Sam, you're running out of time.

Sam You lied to me!

Henri I told you not to build by the motorway.

Sam Two thousand people! What am I supposed to do?

Henri Relocate them before the police do it.

Sam In three days? There's talk of resisting.

Henri Resist the CRS?

Sam They are sick of being moved!

Henri What do you want me to say?

Sam I need to know this won't happen again in two weeks' time.

Henri It won't.

Sam There are no more evictions planned?

Henri No.

Sam Promise me.

Henri There are no more evictions planned.

Mohammed (*to the meeting*) The Sudanese people wish to relocate. We do not want to fight the CRS.

Helene Eritrea also want to relocate.

Ali Kurdistan will relocate.

Omid Iran will move.

Sam These are brave decisions.

Salar The Afghan people wish to resist.

Uproar among the other nationalities.

Mohammed Salar!

Helene We have escaped war. We do not need more!

Ali If Afghanistan resists, then so does Kurdistan. We stand with you, Salar.

Mohammed No, Ali!

Omid Iran will fight too.

Yasin Gaza will resist.

Sam Safi, you need to say something!

Mohammed Poison, Salar! You are no better than the fools we fled from.

Sam I can move your restaurant, Salar. Tomorrow.

Mohammed Please, listen to him.

Sam Wherever you want. It will be exactly the same, I promise.

Salar No.

Sam If you resist, people will die.

Salar It is their will.

Sam So persuade them otherwise.

Salar I cannot force them.

Sam You are their leader!

Salar Just as you cannot force me.

Sam How much have you told them?

Salar Are you accusing me of lying to my people?

Sam They will lose.

Salar 1839. 1888. 2001.

Sam What?

Salar Karz. My village in Afghanistan.

Sam Please.

Salar You know nothing of our struggle. For you, this is good chance. For us, it is our life.

Sam I know I can leave when I want. I know I could be at home with my family. I know I could be anywhere, anywhere but the fucking Jungle. I know that, but I'm not. I am here. I'm still here. I'm still here.

Salar Sam. I built this restaurant with my hands. The roof above your head, the table you are standing on, the benches everyone is sitting at. Everything you see, I found. You think I will watch them destroy my home? I will not move.

Mohammed takes his hands.

Mohammed We looked into each other's eyes on the first day and made a promise.

Salar No, Mohammed –

Mohammed Look at me. We promised to stand together. This restaurant is not this land or this wood. It is us.

You are my friend, and I love you. We have to stand together now.

Pause.

I propose a vote.
  Who wishes to resist?

Around half raise their hands.

Who wishes to co-operate with the relocation?

The other half raise their hands.
  Salar raises his hand too, causing uproar among the Afghan boys.

Salar The Afghan people will relocate.

Sam Thank you.

Salar But my restaurant stays here. Now go.

Safi Salar.

Salar Go!

Sam The majority are in agreement. We have three days. This is our time. Let's show them how we do things here.

Everyone rushes out.
  The Great Move begins.

Salar (*to Norullah*) Go with the black boy, Norullah. Go now!

Salar is left alone with Safi.

Safi This is when my mind becomes muddy. Days pile on top of days on top of days.
  I see a man.
  I see him serving bread and tea in his restaurant near his home, built again in the ruins of his village in Afghanistan. His wife worked with him day after day to open the restaurant.

They had lost two children. One, Zadfar, before he could be born. And one, Leila, in a *tafjeer* . . . A roadside bomb.

A deep grief inside them. The only cure, keep going. Keep working. Keep fighting. Wednesday.

Derek enters.

Derek (*to Salar*) We moved two hundred houses yesterday.

Salar Congratulations.

Derek I've come to tell you that we are moving Afghans west of the dome today.

Salar It is kind of you to come and tell me, Derek.

Derek The police will arrive in thirty-six hours.

Salar They will receive a good welcome when they do.

Safi I see a man who made a promise. To search the earth for a better life. For somewhere possible.
I see my friend . . .
I see an end.
Thursday.

Mohammed enters.

Mohammed All the Afghans have been moved, Salar.

Salar How are they?

Mohammed Everyone on top of each other, different places. Afghans next door to Sudanese. But they are working together. Everyone is working together.

Salar Very good.

Mohammed Please, reconsider. They need this restaurant. They need you.

Salar I won't move. I don't have to explain why.

Mohammed I can't watch this happen.

Salar Thank you for helping my people, Mohammed.

Safi Salar, whether you stand, resist, relocate . . . It is over. You know it. I knew it. We are alone in this world. Strangers to each other. We can only save ourselves.
Why won't you save yourself?
Friday.

Sam enters.

Sam The police are surrounding you.

Ali They have bulldozers.

Salar You know my answer.

Sam This is your last chance.

Salar I have been moved, and moved, and moved, and moved.

Sam We still have time to save the restaurant.

Salar No, Sam. You have a good heart, but it is done. I can't be moved again.

Derek First, they'll ask you to move. If you refuse, they'll try to arrest you. If you resist arrest, they will use force. Do not fight them. If you do, you will lose.

Helene and Norullah enter together, followed by the whole community.

Helene They are here.

Salar You should leave now. Norullah!

Pause.

Helene Give it to him.

Norullah The community make statement.

*He hands a piece of paper to Salar. During this
speech, everyone stands on the tables alongside Salar
in an act of solidarity.*

Salar 'We, the united people of the Jungle, Calais, respect-
fully decline the demands of the French government. We
have moved our houses, we have moved our community,
but we will peacefully resist the government's plans to
destroy our restaurant. We plead with the French
authorities and the international communities that you
understand our situation and respect our fundamental
human right to a place of safety.'

The united people of the Jungle.

They sing.

Thank you, my friends. Thank you.

Safi This restaurant, where we are sat. It was really
many restaurants. Cafés, shops, schools, places. Each
of them a Jungle. And in this story, in my head, this
restaurant is saved. In this moment, it is Afghanistan.
And the people inside it, from Afghanistan, Sudan, Syria,
Eritrea, Iran, Iraq, Kurdistan, Pakistan, Ethiopia,
Kuwait, Egypt, Yemen, Palestine, Nigeria, Mali, Somalia,
Senegal, Germany, America, Spain, Holland, Italy,
Britain, and, yes, some from France, held hands to
defend it.

Great is the hope that makes man cross borders.
Greater is the hope that keeps us alive.

*The CRS enter the restaurant as the residents kneel
defiantly.*

CRS Officer (*French, to the bulldozers outside*) Stop.
Stop.

The officers leave. Blackout.

Ali finds Safi.

Ali Safi! Safi! It's tonight. Eight p.m., lorry park near Guînes. Don't be late. Omid!

Safi We won't. (*To Beth.*) Beth, it's now.

Beth Shit. Okot! Quick, or we'll be late.

Okot Where are we going?

Beth You're going to be in the UK tonight.

Okot No?

Safi He's here.

Beth (*to Okot*) Here's a bag. There are two phones. A torch, hat, gloves. I don't know how cold it will get.

Okot This is not good man.

Safi If he takes you to a refrigerated lorry, don't go inside.

Beth He is going to put you in a good lorry. He is going to get you to UK.

Okot I cannot leave without Norullah.

Beth Don't worry about Norullah, I'll look after him.

Okot He has gun.

Beth This fucking place! You are leaving France tonight. When you get to the UK the first thing you do is find a police station. Tell them your story, exactly like you told me. Tell them you are a child. Tell them you want to claim asylum. This journey, this story. It won't be you any more. This is the hope.

She holds out the bag to him. He doesn't move.

Safi Take the bag.

Ali Take the fucking bag.

He does. Beth hugs him. She can't let go.

Safi Beth, leave.

Ali We have to go.

Safi He'll be fine.

Beth Call me from Leicester.

She leaves.

Ali Quick.

Okot goes to Ali. Safi goes to follow.

Not you, Safi. (*To Okot.*) Wait for me down there.

Ali directs Okot off.

Safi What's going on, Ali?

Ali I only have one.

Safi What do you mean?

Ali I have only have one onion tonight.

He holds it out.

Safi What about the boy?

Ali What about you? You have been a good man.

Pause.
Safi considers . . . and walks towards him.

No guilt.

Safi I'm sorry. I'm sorry.

He snatches the onion.
Ali leaves.

I felt every vibration as the lorry travelled over every
bump and hole in the road. I heard every noise. I panicked

every time the lorry stopped and thought it must be the end. For eighteen hours I stayed quiet, hardly breathing. Then the doors opened. I will never forget the face of the man who opened the box. 'Quickly, mate. You're in England.'

I came to a place called Maidstone and found a police station. My name is Safi Al-Hussain. I have fled Syria and I have fled the Jungle. I would like to claim asylum in UK. And then I handed her my onion.

Salar's restaurant.

Salar They wanted a fight! They wanted to come with their batons and bulldozers. They wanted to destroy the Afghan flag. But we showed them who we are!

Boxer starts the Afghan national anthem. Everyone joins him.

Mohammed We showed them we are together. One country. One Jungle country.

Derek Alright, alright, we've got a lot to get through. Sam?

Sam We moved eight hundred houses. Eight hundred homes. The authorities are satisfied, and I'm confident –

Salar Does that mean no more evictions?

Sam Yes.

Salar Is that a promise?

Sam Yeah. That's a promise.

Huge cheers.

Salar goes over and plants a huge kiss on Sam.

Salar What did I tell you about this boy?!

More music begins.

Derek Thank you. Paula.

Paula The Home Office lost in the High Court. We are going to get every child to safety. The first four children under Dublin III arrive at London St Pancras tomorrow.

More and more people join in the music, it's beginning to completely overwhelm the meeting.

Derek Thank you. Beth.

Beth I also have some good news, I think Okot made it to the UK –

Chants of Yayayayayayayaya!
Maz jumps up to reprise 'Glory, Glory Man United'. Norullah joins him.

Salar Norullah, I need a hundred chickens and six sacks of rice! My restaurant is open!

All My restaurant!

Everyone enjoys this brief reprieve.
Until it ends abruptly.

Safi The southern half of the camp was evicted six weeks later.

One hundred and ninety-eight children went missing, including Okot, and no one saw them again.

Norullah was hit by a lorry on the motorway and was buried, if you remember, in Angel's Corner, a muddy patch at the edge of a graveyard.

Little Amal leads Norullah off.

In October, the north was evicted, and the Jungle was gone.

Now, fields of yellow rape, six feet high, grow in the sand where the Jungle once was. Apart from small footprints, where nothing grows. Where the church stood. Mosques. A restaurant.

And now, my friends, I need a good chance.

I sit here, day after day, in my temporary room in Leicester.

I have been waiting to become a person again, an official refugee. The Home Office are doing the best they can. Unfortunately, my name can be spelt in a number of ways, which makes it hard for them to be sure of who I am, and I cannot yet receive asylum. I cannot work but I am given £36.95 each week, which is generous and I appreciate.

I have two friends in Birmingham who I see sometimes. I walk around Leicester, which is a beautiful city to live in, but sometimes difficult to become a part of. Simple things like how do I find another person here? I spoke more English in the Jungle than I do in England. I feel my heart closing every day.

It takes pain to live side by side. It takes even more to live alone.

He breathes in, looks up.

And now you know.

There are nearly a thousand refugees still living in Calais today. The police prevent any building. Any sign that things might grow again. Volunteers distribute what little they have. Their vans give out meals in car parks, roads, wherever they can.

Thank you for your hospitality.

I hope one day to return to Aleppo. When I do, you are all very welcome.

But to those who were our friends, who are not here now, we think of you. We pray for you. We love you. May peace be with you. And Allah grant you safety and comfort.

The End.